"Heart warming and
Joann Fletcher l   _____aster

"I invited Bill and his son Peter to join my team on the
Eastern Desert Survey expeditions. Our objective was to find
and record ancient rock art in the maze of wadis between the
Nile and Red Sea. *Another Egypt* brings our adventures in
those heady days back to life, a time of great discoveries and
friendships well made"
David Rohl Egyptologist

"*Another Egypt* is a unique and very amusing look at the
modern world's favourite ancient civilization"
Dr Kent Weeks Theban Mapping Project

"Having travelled with Bill I know from experience that he
notices the quirky little episodes that others miss. With his
wonderful insights into human behaviour, *Another Egypt* is a
must read for all fans of Egypt
Janet Shepherd Sussex Egyptological Society

"Bill has captured the sheer joy of travelling in Egypt,
together with the fun to be had with a rich mix of
companions"
Peter Allingham Ancient World Tours

The Author

Bill Dixon grew up in the rural Cotswolds when the sight of a car was a rare thing. He prepared for the Baptist Ministry at Bristol Baptist College and studied theology at Bristol University. He pastored in Birmingham for 28 years, was a member of the Prison Parole Board, and served as Chairman of the Mercian Housing Association. Bill has travelled widely with mentoring projects in South Africa, Malawi, Mozambique, Siberia, Iraq, Albania, Lebanon and California. Now he has pretensions to be an author and a poet. He is married to Jennifer and they have one remaining son, Peter.

ANOTHER EGYPT

Bill Dixon

With thanks for
everything you do.
And best wishes for Surge.

TRANSFORMING CITIES

Bill Dixon

Author photo by Sarah Frost
Taken in The Library of Birmingham

My Inspiration

It is so much pleasanter to please than to instruct, to play the companion rather than the preceptor. What, after all, is the mite of wisdom I could throw into the mass of knowledge? Or, how am I sure that my sagest deductions may be safe guides for the opinion of others? But in writing to amuse, if I fail, the only evil is in my own disappointment. If, however, I can by any lucky chance rub out one wrinkle from the brow of care, or beguile the heavy heart of one moment of sorrow; If I can, now and then penetrate through the gathering film of misanthropy, prompt a benevolent view of human nature, and make my reader more in good humour with his fellow beings and himself, surely, surely, I shall not have then written in vain.

J Arthur Gibbs, 'A Cotswold Village' 1898, quoting Irving Wallace

APOLOGIES

If you happen to recognise yourself it was not you.

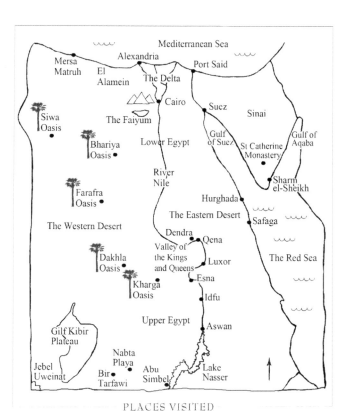

PLACES VISITED

Foreword

By Professor Joann Fletcher, Egyptologist & Broadcaster

Although I first met Bill Dixon on an expedition looking for monuments and mummies in the deserts of Peru rather than the sands of Egypt, we share the idea that travel, even with the most serious of purpose, has to be fun. And in Bill's company, this is indeed the case!

With an ever-present twinkle in his eye, Bill sees the world in his own inimitable way - and this is certainly true of the way in which he sees Egypt.

His descriptions of its beautiful landscapes, friendly people and eccentric travellers are both heart-warming and humorous in turn, and if some of his stories raise a smile and a chuckle, this is exactly the effect Bill's sense of fun has on those lucky enough to travel with him.

His regard for this amazing country and its people can be found throughout this book, creating a wonderful reminder of the land so many of us love, and to which so many of us return, again and again.

Although at the time of writing Egypt is experiencing serious political turmoil, as it moves toward the brighter future its people deserve, the good times will eventually return. Until then, *Another Egypt* is a real memento of one of the world's genuinely special places, and I can certainly recommend it.

University of York, Autumn 2013

Preface

Open in front of me is a book called *1001 Wonderful Things* (edited by Walter Hutchinson, Hutchinson & Co, London, 1935). I gave it to my son, Peter, after purchasing it in a second hand bookshop in Hay-on-Wye. Back in 1944, when I was just ten years old, my father had given me the same book and it was my treasure.

Those days of war were so uncertain. A sniper in WWI had killed my paternal grandfather in a village called Bethune, somewhere near the French/Belgian border, and we were all hoping to get through WWII unscathed. The answer to every question in those days was, 'When the war is over…' and this applied to sweets, oranges and holidays alike.

When Dad had the time he loved to tell me about Howard Carter discovering Tutankhamun's tomb in the Valley of the Kings, and together we would thumb through *1001 Wonderful Things*. My favourite page contained the picture of the *Temple of Abu Simbel*. It was described as a mighty temple in the Sudan, built in the reign of Rameses II. The picture included two statues each sixty-five feet high, representing Rameses II seated in the ceremonious posture of an Egyptian ruler. On his head is the double crown representing Upper and Lower Egypt. Every time I opened the book it was the first picture I saw and I would say, "Dad, one day I'm going there!"

The years passed, our places of habitation changed, and the book got lost.

It was not until 1990, aged nearly sixty, that I was able to make the first of many expeditions to the land of Rameses II, with my son Peter, recording prehistoric rock art with the Easter Desert Survey. We discovered simple swirls and patterns but also exquisite portrayals of animals and people. Gazelle in many guises, cattle, donkeys, ostrich, hippo, crocodile, rhino, lion, cheetah and elephant all grace the desert rocks as once they graced the savannah.

I wanted you to be able to share some of the fun and delight I have experienced travelling in the desert with Peter, and sailing on the Nile with my wife, Jennifer. If you smile or chuckle, I shall consider my task complete.

Desert Deception

You hear them long before you see them. In the stillness and the silence of the desert, all sounds demand attention.

But other sounds get in the way. There is the almost human cry of the Rock Hyrax. Neither the devilish cry of the 'Salawa' which took away naughty children after dark, whose one and only surviving skeleton is said to have been exhibited somewhere at Armant, could capture the attention and curdle the blood like the Rock Hyrax. It screams just when you have made yourself comfortable following the instructions for ablutions, 'gents to the right' and 'ladies to the left.' Messy consequences ensue.

But where was I before the lavatorial reality captured my attention? Ah yes, the magical desert sound. You have to look up, and that can be difficult after days spent looking down studying rock art. When you do look up, limited sky is visible above the vertical wadi walls, so you still cannot see the source. Quickly moving to a better vantage point higher up seems best, and suddenly, there they are!

The brightness of the sun gives their white wings a transparency that only disappears when the black feathers catch the brilliance of desert-reflected sunlight. White storks are migrating. They seek the rising thermals to make their long journey from deepest Africa to their nesting grounds in Europe.

On one notable day, we never saw the roost but it could not have been too far away, many were only a metre or two above the ground. We could not help but see them. Indeed, one seemed almost to brush the laden roof of the Land Cruiser as it struggled to leave the dune ridge. Trying to gauge numbers of these birds in their majestic curtain pattern folds across the sky, stirred a memory that spoke of learning to count birds in batches, say of fifties. So I began and soon was overtaken by the hundreds. There could well have been more than a thousand. Not only did they noise their presence with consistent calls but also, low enough, mute swan like, announced their presence with the sound of beating wing. Shadows on the sand, as beautiful as the silhouettes in the sky, moved in graceful formation. The temptation was to duck and weave, which many of us involuntarily did. The dilemma was where or which way to look. In no time at all it seemed the chequered panoply was gracing the heavens, giving a sense of distance, as small clouds do on a clear blue summers day. Now panoptic for the first time, emotions stirred that said this would soon be over and what had been witnessed would forever be lost. One of nature's greatest spectacles observed, as always, when one is in the right place at the right time.

But not all survive. Deep in the Great Sand Sea, heading for Gilf Kebir and Jebel Uweinat in the south east corner of the country, we stumbled across the abandoned aerodrome known as Eight Bells. Wandering around, uncertain how to photograph a landing strip marked out across the level desert surface with multitudes of two gallon Shell petrol cans, as pristine as the day they were placed and having no elevation to get a higher perspective, there he was. I say 'he', though it could well have been 'she'. Identified by feathers, the white stork lay where he fell, blown hundreds of kilometres off course. How long he had lain there undisturbed was impossible to estimate. There was a sense of anticipation about him as though awaiting the arrival of an avian hearse to gently lift his form and with due consideration convey him to a place of respectful safety, to await a ritual burial. No scavenger had disturbed his long desiccated form. Neither had the sand attempted to conceal his modesty. He lay as deserted as the aerodrome and maybe he was the last to come down this long forgotten flight path, never to achieve elevation again. Yet there was more. On closer inspection of the beak, bone, and feathers, the eye was drawn to a stranger in the crop. There, nestling in its death bed was a frog, of equal desiccation and state of preservation, undigested, a companion in death.

Birds Hold a Fascination

I would feel as if I were naked should I have to travel without my binoculars. Birds have always held a fascination for me ever since I grew up in the countryside before and during World War II. The larger ones, like pigeon, partridge, and pheasant you ate, anything smaller you watched. I guess it was my father who, teaching me how to use the double-barrelled four-ten shotgun, introduced me to the world of wildlife and birds, in particular.

A great delight of mine is to walk slowly through the halls of Luxor Temple in the evening, when the floodlights give it that ethereal glow. Have you ever noticed the fleeting shadows and the gentle cries of the Little Owls who make their homes in the crevices atop the pylons?

Another joy is to let the felucca, that modern descendant of the early Nile sailboat gently drift on the current, to gain close proximity to the many waders that inhabit banks, even beside the many moored river cruisers. Then to sail the reaches and head to the far side, opposite Banana Island, there to lie in wait for the beautiful Little Bee Eaters to dance their pirouettes against an azure sky. Walking the Western Valley in the Valley of the Kings is an experience not to be missed. As you look to the cerulean sky, an optical illusion gives the cliff tops an overlay of soft blue haze through which the Pale Crag Martins weave and dive. The deserts too have their own avifauna that, like the Nile Valley itself, hosts at migration seasons many species that are simply passing through. It is at such times that the most elementary bird book can prove inadequate and the more comprehensive too heavy to hold.

Reflect for a moment on the freedom of these birds compared with our own limitations. To visit Egypt we need a visa. To leave the city we have to join a convoy. To visit the desert we need a permit and still we find some access denied. No, I am not complaining, just observing. The physical barriers for birds are determined by the rules of nature, whilst ours bring into play a plethora of emotion, an embarrassment of prejudice, and an excess of conceit. With boundaries disputed and borders protected we set about determining each other's territorial confines with a zeal exhibited in war, conquest and enslavement.

Just after the shock and awe visited upon Baghdad prior to the invasion by the international forces led by the Americans, helping to alleviate some suffering and having with me the ever-present binoculars, I looked for birds and found them too, free of all constraints, mindful of no political or religious divides. They took no sides, observed no impositions, and freely crossed all man-made barriers to be at home and at peace in the place of their own choosing. Should the privilege be given to return in another life, the longing of all Egyptian Ancients, for me the choice would be simple, it would have to be a bird. Should you press me as to species, it would be the Peregrine Falcon. Then I would be free to move from place to place needing neither permission nor permit.

The Jacuzzi

No, it is not new! Nature, not man created the prototype. Wadi Umm Salam, hidden in Egypt's Eastern Desert, is a place of deep peace, beauty, and until recent times, undiscovered art that can be ranked alongside the finest in the world. For canvas, rock surface; for artist's instrument, a harder stone; for topic, all that has passed before. Perhaps with casual disdain an ancestor picked up a stone and rubbing it against a softer one, saw that it etched a mark, then tapped a stone on rock and saw that it made a patination, then began to represent what his eye could see. But he was not the first to sculpt design. Nature came before him. Standing on the wadi floor, looking at the towering cliffs above, the dramatic rock formation cried out to tell me something of its ancient history.

To the left was a normal wadi wall, (if there is ever such a thing), and pecked upon it was found an enigmatic swirl with a prehistoric feel about it. Likewise, to the right a similar rock formation is presented. Hidden in the light and shade are some boat impressions. In between, what drama has occurred to create this cacophony of rock formation with horizontal and vertical faces at contorted angles, precariously poised as if to fall at any moment? Yet fall they did millennia ago, when rain on plains above descended in tropical downfalls year on year. Guided by some tantalising force of fate, the contours gathered waters from some vast expanse and sent them cascading down the rock wall, creating a chasm in this already pre-formed gully. With persistence, year on year the waters carved their path, until some softer rock, worn by the mingled stone and water, gave way and the under-cutting began. How long it took for the chaos to be caused, who could guess, but came the day when all support below was gone and crashing down, upended by the power, the horizontal rock came to rest in a vertical and angular display. So it stood from age to age, until that day when I beheld the wonder and the beauty and saw that sand had filled the crevices where wind-weathered rock allowed it to be retained.

Between that far-off day and my arrival, many had come before, from early man and pastoralist, to pharaonic precursor, then those of that amazing civilisation itself. No doubt some Greeks and Romans, Blemeys (the nomadic Nubian tribe who long fought the Romans from the late 3rd century on) and those leading the Arab invasion came down this way too, for all have left their tell tale marks. My purpose though is different. I am here to discover and record the past, not to mould the present.

So I begin the climb and after attaining three or four metres above the sandy floor I find an unexpected turn that almost takes me back upon myself. There before me, previously hidden, an almost vertical wall of rock, some ten metres tall and at least six wide, covered with layer over layer of man and beast, pecked with beauty and precision. Dominating all, three mighty giraffe stand proud, each two or three metres tall. Just how did men or women stand to reach so high, where today all signs of visible support are gone? Now my curiosity is really stimulated and I begin a more rigorous search of the rocks already climbed. It pays to concentrate on one activity at a time in some of these precarious positions! All around were people, dogs, cattle and gazelle, intimately carved but for whom to see and admire?

But still above was more. Letting the rock contours lead me left and right, higher and higher, nothing prepared me for what I saw next. To my surprise it was below me. A huge circular excavation that contained some small debris that time had contributed, accompanied by three large rounded boulders. It was these that had been the excavators as, on looking up yet again, there before me was the evidence. The waters had cascaded down, and first only imperceptibly, begun a circular motion. Over time this had accelerated, but how many hundreds of years had elapsed to carve this whirlpool of such amazing dimensions? Water and rock combined to create a hole, at least four metres across and three metres deep which quite easily contained our whole party for the inevitable 'Group Photo' of about twenty-five people.

Before everyone was called to see the amazing 'Jacuzzi' as I called it, there remained two things for me to do. First to explore above to see the worn watercourse across the ridge, that had worked this miracle of nature and it was whilst there that I discovered the second. Looking down on the Jacuzzi from above, the sunlight exposed the rim about 20cms wide and there emerging in feint detail was something carved. I had to go down into the waterless Jacuzzi and find some foothold to raise me to a point where I might discover detail. Now I could see how beautiful they were. With what pride they had been worked out and only from within the pool could the artist have applied his amazing skill. So my imagination saw him, up to his waist in cool water, standing on the very foothold I was now employing, looking way down to the wadi floor where tethered to prevent them wandering, were his prize bovines. Day after day he came up here and carved the herd, for his own delight. Their horns, patterned skin and proportioned udders were delicately picked out as they processed around the rim of nature's Jacuzzi. Being long dead, now they live in stone, just for me, and of course for you.

White Desert, Sand and Snakes

No lunar landscape could match the beauty of the White Desert. To wear the latest sunglasses would be to destroy the intensity of colour and light, though some could not be persuaded to take them off. It is as though beneath the brilliance of vast blue sky and above the tortured turmoil of the land, some vast sieve filled with icing sugar had been gently shaken. All is coated in such a delicate white sand that if you lick your finger, dip it in the dust, then let it brush your lips, on tasting it will be the sweetest thing on earth.

Apparently, it is the wind that has eroded chalk to create surreal forms but even that might not satisfy the geologist in you and certainly will never satisfy the poet, or even me. With each passing hour, the sun acquiring a new apogee as the earth relentlessly revolves, gives to the scene a different refracted light and colour. It remains the same only for moments. It is predominantly shades of silver and gold that are seen by day. The magic however really begins when earth-rise gives the sensation of a setting sun. All the pastel shades, from violet through pink emerge as the scene changes yet again. White has given way to gold, has given way to mauve and still the panoply is not exhausted for yet the moonlight has to weave its wonders. Now it is the turn of monolithic ghosts that seem to sway and topple, yet remain upright to haunt those lingering overnight. In the Sahara it is difficult to imagine a more Antarctic scene, save underfoot is sand not ice. And about the underfoot we were duly warned.

All creatures leave traces of their passing and one to be avoided is that of the scorpion. I had no knowledge of what it was like until the day I pitched my tent too close to some warm rocks and a beautiful yellow-green diaphanous creature came out to investigate the commotion on his campus. Quickly he hurried back to the shelter of his cave rightly assuming that I presented no threat to him. He did however leave a trail so distinct and clear that I have never forgotten it.

Another creature of which to take great care is the snake. I am told sidewinders like this awesome desert and knowing from 'Discovery TV' what trail they leave, I looked and looked but all in vain. Now in my wandering, a little way away from my congenial companions, I found some twigs, left I supposed from some campfire fuel gathered and brought from some other place. What caught my eye was the four-pronged end of this particular kindling and in my mind a plan was hatched. A little later a cry went up from a clearly alarmed member of our party. The voice was high pitched and echoed through the stillness: "Be careful over here! Fresh sidewinder tracks. An adult and three young."

Disappearance of Dakhla

You see the escarpment a long way off. I just thought high cliffs but as we gradually came closer, something far more magnificent came into view. Rising on average over 600 metres, these sculpted curtains form a northern backdrop to the greenness of new cultivation. Colours reminiscent of Jordanian Rhum and Petra came to mind as the sun unveiled new contours hidden in the shade.

The traditional picture of an oasis as being a pool and palm trees does not prepare you for their sheer size. In some cases habitation is scattered over a hundred kilometres and there is a distinct hierarchy for each community. There can also be a 'capital', in this case Mut, for this is Dakhla Oasis.

I guess you could say it was hot. Hot and humid. We had been warned about mosquitoes too but such was our excitement that we took little notice of what was being said by way of caution. It was the thought of the hot pools that came with such recommendation that now captured our attention. Depositing our meagre desert travel chattels, we headed off with towels and trunks. The clear water of Cleopatra's Pool at Siwa spoils you for what you find in the mineral-infested hot springs of other oases. It is a colour that clings to you. Rising from the pool you are tempted to make use of the towel and undertake a quick rub down. Looking at others you suddenly realise that you are in the same predicament as they. Iron brown I call it, too bold for rust but I think that is being very kind. Quickly, skin and trunks are dried in the heat and after evening refreshment you wonder if it is getting warmer still. Minimal clothing and damp towels do not do an adequate job of cooling and after that, time to relax, and whose turn is it?

That I shall have to explain. It begins when the rituals of check in and security at the airport are over. It's usually Heathrow for the scheduled Egypt Air flight of 'meat or fish?' fame. That is the cabin crews' constant call as the refreshment trolleys are wheeled into service. But for the present, 'World of Whiskey' is the destination and each traveller selects his choice tipple for the desert expedition. In that way we get to share each other's tastes and are thus introduced to new Single Malts or abysmal Blends, with the bland taste to some sad palettes. So, turn and turn about, we do our best to share, with varying degrees of success.

Now back to Dakhla, where a new Single Malt is being sampled. One by one we drift away to our appointed places of repose to fight the heat and mosquitoes with the mistaken soporific powers of the fermented grain. Who was last to leave? I've no idea but it was my bottle and in the morning it is not there upon the table. Each in turn is asked where they have put it but all deny responsibility. There is only one conclusion that can be drawn. The bottle was not empty and it has been 'nicked'. "Leave it to me," is the Team Leaders reassurance and I am left to wonder if he knows something that we do not. Later he arrives, secure with the missing bottle and to all intents and purposes, little has been consumed.

"So where was it?" we enquire.

"It was quite safe," comes the reply, "in the keeping of the local inspector of constabulary."

A Fayoum Experience

Called Lake Qaroun, this is not an oasis in the strictest sense. It is a vast expanse of water in the desert that conveniently provided the depression into which through canal and ditch, the Nile has been diverted at various times through the Millennia. Now less then a quarter of its original size and a mere forty metres lower, the water level is still subject to fluctuation. The increasing salinity thus caused has spelled doom for all fresh water fish so, ever resourceful, the fishing industry has stocked it with various sea-going varieties. There is however, another problem that the changing water level has caused and that concerns those living on the shoreline. Sometimes they are left high and dry and sometimes they are flooded. Sea defences is far too grand a concept but attempts have had to be made in more recent times to keep the water from some hotels and homes as the lake remains undecided what its confines should be.

The Hotel Auberge du Lac-Fayoum has something of an illustrious history. It was once King Farouk's hunting lodge and another of its claims to fame is that it hosted the Allied and Arab leaders conference after World War II where the Middle East was again carved up among competing nations. Now somewhat jaded, it stands below the current level of the lake and could well be in danger of getting its foundations wet. Such fear sprang to mind during my experience staying there.

It was a very pleasant room and after being shown around by a very fussy porter angling for a larger tip, I looked at my holdall bag on its stand and decided against opening it straight away. Sampling the well appointed en-suite bathroom had to take precedence. Having pulled the flush I returned to the task of settling in and after some moments, hearing the flush still working, I took a cautious look behind me. Coming from under the door was water, seeping on to the carpet! Was it the plumbing or the lake? A quick call to reception brought an unhurried response and I ventured back to the offending cistern to see if I could do anything to stem the flow. Unfortunately not. The workman came, splashed about and implemented some sort of repair with which he seemed all too familiar. His English and my Arabic were insufficient to glean much but I gathered he had put the problem right but had not tested it. Looking round to give a cursory inspection of his skill, I found to my dismay, that he had disappeared. My dilemma now was should I test his workmanship or leave it, in case the same thing happened again? My decision was to test it, and gingerly I splashed through an inch or so of water to locate the flush. Summoning all my courage I pulled the lever down. Of course it would be all right. The flush began to work and the tank began to fill but unfortunately there was no stopping the flow and once again the depth of water round my feet began to rise. 'Below the water level of the lake,' was the fact that flashed across my mind again. I was left wondering if all this was the fault of Bahr Yusef, he of Old Testament fame, if he had indeed ordered the first construction of the canal from the Nile to the lake.

The Great Adventure

You have to cross the great Gilf Kiber, if your destination is Jebel Uweinat, approaching from the north (and ours definitely was). On the way we climbed Abu Ballas, the Hill of Pots, to view previously recorded rock art and spy out the land for a prospective campsite. The Gilf Kiber itself is a huge plateau about the size of Switzerland, with a steep escarpment running down the western edge. Descent is afforded in only one place, the Wadi Al Aqaba. Riding down it in a Land Cruiser is an awesome experience, sliding from side to side, watching cliff faces flash past. Ascent is almost impossible but we do read that explorers managed it in the 1930s with two wheel drive Fords!

We had other problems. Daklah Oasis was the site of the last filling station and we had taken on board supplies of diesel, but no one at the time knew it was contaminated. The cook's van was the first to show signs of trouble. It spluttered along very slowly, then it flew down the pass very impressively, but the next day, on the flat, it gave out altogether. Resourceful as the desert drivers are, they carry strong towropes.

Setting out towing the cook's van proved to be no problem and so we continued on our way. From time to time the drivers in the desert like to overtake each other, though there is usually a very strict order to be followed. Sometimes for terrain reasons, it becomes impossible to observe the rules, hence it was no surprise when on our left we saw another vehicle beginning to overtake. Looking at the speedometer I was surprised to see it registering just over one hundred, but imagine my astonishment to see that not only were we being overtaken by another Land Cruiser but also by the cook's van! The cook's face must have been a picture.

Eventually we had to abandon that cook's van and distributed his utensils and supplies among the other 4x4s. How the cook loved sitting in such close proximity to the female punters. Opportunity provided by our misfortune, proved to be a blessing to him. Later, we were to discover he had other hidden talents, namely changing wheels, for we had a total of eleven punctures on that trip.

We were to experience more misfortune than a record number of punctures on one trip. The Dirty Diesel of Daklah, as it became known, soon struck again. Losing the use of another Land Cruiser meant a decision from the commander in chief was called for, should we go on or turn back? There really was no way we could continue abandoning vehicles in the deep desert, though we did wonder who was there in the desert to cannibalise them whilst they were awaiting retrieval. Some unsuspecting explorer might yet come across our Marie Celeste of the great sand sea.

The decisive decision was made and we set out for home, passing en route the monument erected to commemorate the exploits of explorer Prince Kamal al-Din. Hidden in the monument, in a carefully concealed recess is an ancient tin, in which by tradition, wayfarers passing that way leave a note. On opening the tin we found it about half-full of notes so there was plenty of space for our contributions. What a privilege to place a brief note alongside those of much more historic significance.

So our brief excursion into the deep desert was nearly at its abandoned end but not quite. Moving rapidly over some smooth terrain, quite suddenly we came upon almost invisible dips in the sands with corresponding ridges, about eighteen inches deep. The first three vehicles in front met them at speed. We watched as they danced high prior to their sudden descent and then we too joined in the shindig. Seated in the front seat of the fourth vehicle, I semi stood and yelled but it was too late. Most heads hit the roof and as the seat came up to meet the descending posteriors, at speed, they hit the roof a second time. Apart from one back that was given quite a workout, the rest of the team seemed unhurt. However, when the vehicles came to a stand still, the cook bounded out and rushed around to the back of his assigned vehicle. We all shouted warnings that he should only open the door slowly but he was too eager to assess the damage. As he jerked it free his precious consignment of eggs cascaded onto the sand where they fried on impact.

So often, when you are in the heart of nowhere, help is never far away. At Bir Tarfawi there is a remote outpost of the Egyptian Army, within which we were but a day's drive, according to our ancient maps. Those soldiers were some of the most hospitable people we met. They looked after us as though we were foreign dignitaries on an official visit. We were escorted to the commander's reception room where we were able to recline on beautifully embroidered settees. Cold fresh fruit juice was offered, whilst by far the most appreciated offer was the use of the officer's facilities. Everything was put at our disposal including the ramp to drain the contaminated fuel and replace it with fresh diesel. All filters were cleaned and soon we were ready to draw a memorable journey to a conclusion. For those who follow us, the Aqaba Pass is not mined as some guide books suggest.

Nabta Playa

I like to think that Nabta Playa, the kidney-shaped desert depression formed by a lake bed from prehistoric times, just sixty kilometres to the northwest of Abu Simbel, should have another name. I would like to christen it Wendorf's Garden, for he it is who has dug it over and cared for it as though it were the most precious plot of land upon the earth. (Fred Wendorf, the Henderson-Morrison Professor emeritus of Anthropology at Southern Methodist University, USA, received his Ph.D. in 1953 from Harvard University. He founded the anthropology department at SMU along with the Fort Burgwin Research Centre in Taos, New Mexico).

To get to Nabta Playa as we did, you take the desert road way south until you come to the last police checkpoint. It was here that we ran into our first problem, but you might not. It was our arrival time that seemed to be the problem. Paper work was fine but it was down to who should see it. Apparently he was asleep. It was his afternoon siesta time and no junior officer had the authority to wake him up. With varying degrees of patience we waited. We had no other choice. That we should be the only people to pass that way for a week or more and ours the only papers he would see during that time, did not matter. He was in charge and we surely had to know it. Wake him at your peril! At last he awoke, and we were released to find an un-signposted left turn into dunes and rocky outcrops away from the setting sun.

A strong wind was blowing when we arrived at another

long forgotten checkpoint in the middle of the desert. We watched as an official 'anorak' jotted down our vehicle registration number in this god-forsaken place, and then he had the ill luck to let go of his piece of paper. It set off with a mind of its own across the desert, with the anorak in hot pursuit. It travelled faster than he could run. All we could do was watch the fun. As paper paused upon the ground awaiting his arrival, just before he could grasp it, off it went again. He ran over a kilometre before his hand held it firm. We had a long wait for his return, but it was a price worth paying.

Heading off again, some white tents in the distance indicated that we were approaching the 'dig' and as always we moved forward with caution and respect. As this was a trip to reconnoiter for future visits, we had no idea what kind of reception we might get. There was an air of stillness about the place and it looked for all the world like a ghost encampment. No people, just the wind disturbing tied canvas. Had we come in the wrong season? Were we too early or too late? It could not be, for there were tables all in place and what looked like archaeological accoutrements scattered around. We drew up and waited.

Sure enough he soon appeared, the little man in the blue galabeya. There was an animated conversation with our guide and soon we were all party to what was going on. Some sort of accident had happened a few days before and a colleague had died. All had left the dig and returned home so the whole site was deserted, save for this lonely caretaker. We took pity on him. Our guide instructed one of our drivers to give him some provisions. It so happened that this driver was one who seemed always to be hungry for he was constantly eating, to such an extent that we changed his name from Ahmed to Snackmed. Following a long search though our stores Snackmed produced just two oranges and duly made a show of presenting them to our hungry-looking host, whereupon our guide seemed subject to some kind of fit. He screamed at poor Snackmed, and though we could not understand the Arabic, we knew full well what was being said. Returning to the store, this time he produced a more substantial offering and without a sign of grace or goodwill thrust it at the poor man. Snackmed would yet have the final word for as we drove away he turned towards the tents, knocked over the tables and ran over the poor man's tools.

Sand Storm at Bahrain Oasis

Siwa Oasis possesses an attribute that is powerful and compelling. It casts a spell on the visitor with the result that some internal irritant constantly demands return. It is Berber North Africa that sets this place apart. Its ruins and archaeology hint at its historical significance, but above all the people are so warm and hospitable they make you feel you belong. To access the area still requires a desert adventure, but it is one that I recommend.

On this particular trip, it was departure along the desert road towards Bahariya Oasis that provided the entertainment. At a remote army checkpoint in the middle of nowhere, we turned right and drove on trackless sand up and over dunes, until a gentle descent brought water into view, fringed with reeds and undergrowth preventing access, which was just as well as the sand was prone to give way and any mosquitoes were best left undisturbed. The water would probably be saline through evaporation.

This was Bahrain Oasis, uninhabited since Roman times. The evidence for this was plain to see, for high on the escarpment that separates the oasis into two lakes, hence its name, was the cemetery where they buried their dead. On arrival, we all looked around for the most propitious place to site our tents as this would be the first night of the trip under canvas.

Those who claimed experience through Scouts and Guides, hurried to their chosen places whilst the rest of us looked around and found some sheltered spots. Dinner preparations were soon underway which gave time for exploration, but not before the ritual warnings from our leader. The dangers of trying to explore the waters edge were pointed out, as was the risk associated with the Roman tombs. It was this latter explanation that was of greatest interest. The rock-carved tombs were open to the elements and the contents quite visible but woe betide us if the dead were disturbed, for some malevolent guardian might visit his wrath upon us. Some headed to the water, others the tombs.

It was the tombs that beckoned me. Soft sand made for a hard climb but my hard work was soon rewarded. Those rock recesses displayed whitened bones and skulls protruding from the sand together with remains of their white linen wrappings. The photographers began their work composing artistic pictures of the dead. Looking around, a magnificent panorama of the desert was now revealed. It dawned on me that this was a most congenial spot to be laid to rest, slid into the rock niche, head first, with feet adorning the entrance. Should some resurrection event overcome you, the first view would be an inspiration. Just how many dead might be laid to rest in the side of this and the surrounding rock facades, it would be hard to estimate, but a cursory count could take you to in excess of fifty. The call for dinner was a welcome invitation, particularly for those who already had experience of the driver's culinary capabilities.

The fall of darkness was abrupt, exposing the brightness of the night sky, free of all light pollution. Tiredness overtook the party and it was clear it was not the time to engage in lengthy stargazing. Silence descended, only to be shattered by the cacophony of snores that kept me awake.

I was away in the far distance of my childhood, where my bedroom window was next to a galvanised tin roof, and the beating rain regularly woke me. There however, the similarity ended. I was wide-awake in my tent and the beating sound was on its plastic skin. It took a few moments to realise what was going on. Sand, not rain must be creating the commotion. The soft warm comfort of the sleeping bag cocooned me in security and I tried to turn to sleep again. It was then I heard a cry. It sounded like a woman in distress.

To respond would be to face the driving sand that could penetrate all the impossible as well as the possible places, but there was no alternative. I wrestled free of the sleeping bag and struggled to put on more respectable clothing from a kneeling position, then exited my tent, securing the flaps behind me. Some of those who had earlier boasted experience of erecting tents now had their lack of ability exposed. The sandstorm had brought destruction on them. Hurriedly we heaped sand around tent walls, providing some temporary shelter from the sand storm, and offered kind words to those who were afraid and exhausted.

With great relief we saw the sun rise. The breath-taking desert dawn was a new experience for some in the party and on reflection they felt it was worth staying awake for. The inevitable executive decision was then taken that we should abandon camp and seek the security of the 4x4s.

We endeavoured to retrace our steps to find the remote army post where we had turned right in the bright sunlight of the day before, but the sand storm had done its work. There were no tyre tracks for us to follow.

We were quite amazed and very relieved to find that army post again. The welcome we received was overwhelming. Shelter was offered, beds given up, cigarettes and food made available, and our party gave tapes of the latest songs in exchange, (though the soldiers were already the proud possessors of Celine Dion's repertoire). The majority of the soldiers were of university education, all the way from Cairo. Some interesting conversations were shared as we enjoyed the richness of desert hospitality. But now the time had come. Who had disturbed the dead bringing retribution raining down as sand upon our heads? Had someone taken a fragment of bone or removed the wrappings of the dead? Had the time come for everyone to be subjected to a search? All I know is that the beating sand of that most memorable night did achieve what I had feared. For many days the places of impossibility gave up their grains of sand.

Wadi Midric Mystery Map

The Wadi Midric is many kilometres long but never more than a few metres wide. There is no possibility of vehicular access, which means everything must be explored on foot. The flood plain that created the wadi in distant prehistoric times is vast. It still collects today's sparse rainfall and directs the surface water down the wadi creating flash floods that can be very dangerous. Witness the debris pushed as high as three metres in places. Cautious in selecting campsites, our team decided that near the wadi entrance but on the edge of the flood plain, would be the wisest place.

After setting up, we walked the few metres to the rising rock face and found it covered with rock art. Tomorrow held out much promise. Ever ones to explore, soon after breakfast, giving no heed to plans as yet unmade, some headed for the rocks and clambered up while the rest of us loitered down below and just waited. By now, one of those on the rocks appeared from our vantage point to be on the skyline and then he disappeared around a boulder. Suddenly a shout of, "Map!" echoed down and we looked up.

Now there is something of a standing joke among us. When you think you have found something of interest you just shout 'Map!' To actually find rock art, which is apparently an ancient map of the surrounding land, is a wonderful discovery to make. (Strange as it may seem we think we may have recorded four out of five new maps though we were not the first to float the idea). So, when we heard the call of "Map!" our response was not overly enthusiastic. We thought it was another joke. Yet there was a real persistence about this call, so with some reluctance we too, began the climb. It is not what is in front of you that you want to take pleasure in when you climb, more often it is the view that is behind, though should you ignore that which is in front you may never live to see the delight of that which is behind. Looking for rock art confirms this, as the rock surfaces are the subject under scrutiny. What we were about to see would give equal weight to those opposing directions.

Reaching the top we turned, stood and looked in awe at the landscape before us, a segmented vista of over two hundred degrees. To the right a vast plain and to the left a narrow rock funnel forming the wadi mouth. The early morning sun caught the pastel green of the young growth vegetation, gathered where the water had pushed the seeds in swathes that now marked out each ebb and flow of surface water running towards its destiny. Months before we arrived (we estimated about six), the mountain watershed along the western Red Sea coast had caused the clouds to release rain that watered an arid landscape that may not have been as damp in ten years or more. Had this been savannah, with the richness of its pasture, it would have supported herds of great African mammals as inhabit the plains further south on this great continent, along with hippos and rhinoceros. Bovines too, herded and tethered would have been there. How do we know? Because with consummate skill the watching herdsmen had depicted it all upon the rock on which we were leaning and which now demanded our attention.

Standing a metre and a half high and the same in width, it was about two metres long. Where the depiction over-ran a block of rock it continued down the side. It just has to be a map. It could be nothing else. No doodle has such precision of repeating what you see before you. There is the plain with certain positions marked and there is the wadi clearly sketched with places marked which might have been wells. If you had been given the task of defending territory or watching game and maybe later herding animals, then this was the vantage point above all others. How long had it been used? Not too far away and hidden by this promontory are remains of shelters. Scattered around on the ground are flints and tools and pottery. Our job is to take the coordinates and leave to others the task of date and provisional assessment.

Alexandria

History was the selling point of the Hotel Cecil, with the names of former guests on its Roll of Honour Board such as Lawrence Durrell, Winston Churchill, Noel Coward, and Somerset Maugham. All added to the ambiance from which renovation distracted. All however, was compensated for by the location with its views of the Eastern Harbour.

Every morning, quite early, I'd meet with friends at reception and walk some of the Corniche. To be beside the sea, smell the fish, watch the boats, chat, and dream of the history, this was our delight.

What is remarkable about this ancient city is that a good half of its archaeological remains are under the sea and only those with the right permission, permits and expertise can access them. Heads, obelisks and monoliths and well over 2500 stone objects lie below water with but a few brought to the surface.

The anticipated visit to Fort Qaitbey would, we hoped, bring us up to date with all that was going on under water as our guest lecturer was also a diver on the project. That wonder of the ancient world, the Pharos Lighthouse, graced this approach to the magnificent harbour in far off time but unlike the wonder of the Pyramids it is no longer to be seen. Standing on the very site had limited compensation to offer. However, this is the place to go to get a proper perspective of this unique city. The other option would be a vessel, either anchored or passing by, to unfold the panorama unsurpassed by any other cityscape.

As with most travellers, who since the invention of

photography, have sought to take home visual memories, so we too armed with the latest 'stills' and videos, began to assess position and composition, to capture the wonder that is Alexandria. Not to be, alas. In bold lettering were the stern commands, 'NO PHOTOGRAPHS'. It seems as though this now dilapidated fort still has some military significance but just what that might comprise is anyone's guess. So time to take stock and assess the possibilities. In front were our guides and with them 'security.' Behind us were more 'security' but looking much more relaxed. Could we take a chance and get away with some discreet picture taking? There were some smokers in the party who were encouraged to gather in a group and create a little convocation by which the video could be screened. Success was gained at one level but alas not at another. The much sought after picture had been captured but so had we! Security, unseen as we went about our business, realised what was going on, probably by dint of much previous experience. We got the impression they might have set the whole thing up. Would we now face camera confiscation or even a visit to their cells? Things turned out to be much simpler. This was the way they kept themselves supplied with western cigarettes and when the fine had been paid with the white weed we were free to continue our exploration.

The Garden

Few do not feel the compulsion to explore the Winter Palace Hotel, to sit at sundown sipping a favourite palliative or to walk the gardens, pool gaze, or climb the circling stairs and walk the halls.

On the other hand, in the intensity of heat, few will pay the price of singular discomfort and don full dress for dinner.

The New Winter Palace Hotel introduces guests to the experience of its illustrious predecessor in a very genteel way. Its approach though air-conditioned comfort and its spacious dining areas give an air of considered opulence and its culinary achievements rank with the best.

However it was the gardens that captivated me for they displayed features that I had never seen before. Early every morning, there was leisured activity in them. I'm sure the gardeners had a circuit to work to. Watering, sweeping, cutting and raking were done and that was only on the lawn. Floodlights were carefully covered to avoid the water spray and all was closely monitored by a colony of House Crows. I felt for those men and wondered how long some of them had been doing this task. Was there a scheme for them to participate in the tipping system of the hotel and did they have a neatly manicured and watered garden in New Gurna on the West Bank from whence many of them hailed? It was my wife who pointed out the absence of flowers for such an extensive garden. Minute borders gave little scope for colourful planting though I guess there would be seasons when we would have been surprised.

A day or two had passed before I realised just what was so different about this garden; it was a neighbour on the next balcony, who started chatting, that began the thought chasing round my mind. He pointed out the carefully coiffured palm trees, their trunks carved with footholds to assist the climber. Though in Jamaica I have seen men take off their boots and walk up trunks as tall as this, to spin the coconuts and let them fall, with no footholds carved for them. Even as we looked out from our third floor room, the palms went on to tower above us, straining for the sky. Yes, the difference was dawning and my mind began to grasp it. With such abundance of palm this amazing garden was taller than it was long.

Keeper of the Golden Mummies

To be around just after the Golden Mummies were discovered, was to live in exciting days. There was a buzz about Bahariya Oasis and exaggerated talk of expansion for the tens of thousands of visitors who would be flocking to see, 'the greatest discovery in the whole of Egypt since Tut'. But aren't they all?

Full of excitement we drove out to the desert site thinking we might be introduced to the donkey whose foot had been the key to the whole discovery when it stumbled, disclosing the hole in the ground penetrating the tomb's decaying ceiling. We did hear that there was a shortage of donkeys for a time, as everybody wanted one to ride out across the desert to make more discoveries. They were in greater demand than metal detectors.

The Keeper's Hut was minimal, the introductions were brief. There was special emphasis placed upon what a privilege was ours to be among the first to see a little of this amazing discovery. There was a donkey close to the keeper's lodge but I forgot to ask if he was the fortunate beast and whether he was being accorded any special honours. We walked for some distance before coming to the hole in the ground, now supported by some rough cut timbers. It grew darker as we descended steps and turned our torches on.

With the ranks of stacked mummies reaching above waist height on either side, we walked through the narrow corridor they formed. With the keeper's flickering torchlight glinting on gold, we stood amazed at what surrounded us.

The smell was not so pleasant and reminded me of a visit to an undertakers walk-in deep freeze back home in Birmingham, built to incredible dimensions to help satisfy the planners' demand, that should a major disaster overtake our city, they would have enough cold storage to contain the dead.

Reaching daylight again we scanned the desert, realising that just below the surface, acre upon acre contained hundreds and hundreds of mummies similar to the ones we had seen. The Keeper joined us in the 4x4s and excitedly told us about his little museum where several of the mummies were stored in glass cases and could be viewed in better light and circumstance. They were exquisite. Their photos have gone around the world. Those of the children, whose small mummies were equal in every respect to the adults, were particularly poignant. What could be learned from this vast cemetery about the life and times of this oasis in the Greco-Roman period? So many were born here, this was their homeland. Most would never have known another. A far-flung outpost of an Empire.

It was whilst at these commandeered agricultural sheds now serving another purpose, that I became aware of the Keeper's ministrations. No matter where I stood he always seemed to be standing next to me. Shaking hands became an embrace and kiss upon each cheek. From time to time the hand upon my shoulder descended to the small of my back. Loath as I was to leave the mummies I was glad to get away from the Keeper as my colleagues will testify!

Dendera Temple

The destination of the small cruise boat 'Lotus' is Qena, provincial capital and the cleanest city in the whole of Egypt. Certainly if you approach by road, men sweeping the verges are much in evidence, down what used to be the 'Mubarak Avenue', reminiscent of an older Avenue of Sphinx. Rumour has it that the Mayor was offered a substantial transfer fee to move to Cairo but the salary did not match the challenge. There was also a whisper that paint was free if you wanted to decorate your home, however, the colour would depend upon your district.

Travelling on board the 'Lotus' is a much more leisurely and sedate way to arrive, though you don't get to see much of the fine architecture and the majestic mosque, with its tomb of a twelfth-century sheikh. But, of course your destination is Dendera and the fine Temple of Hathor.

Especially built on the north side of the Qena Bridge you will find a spacious, landscaped, picturesque and floral series of mooring stages for the cruise boats that venture this far up or down the Nile. There is however one small problem. The level of water in the river limits access to this magnificent government-guarded zone, for all the boats have to pass beneath the bridge. At such times as a higher flow of water is released far south at the great Aswan Dam, the river rises to a level that prevents access. The old dilapidated site to the south of the bridge is used again and here air-conditioned coaches await their customers.

She just could not sit still. Moving from one side of the boat to the other, with the ever-present camera in her hand, she gave the impression of hovering. It was the umbrella that caught the eyes of most. Sympathetically, I assume she has some kind of allergy to the sun, for on her head she wore a hat, which was held in place by a fine cotton scarf. Brightly coloured trousers and a plain blouse were overlaid with a long dress that might have buttoned the full length had it not been so hot. Then there were the calf-length boots! Access for the sunshine was totally denied. Sitting on the wicker chair next to me, at least with the umbrella furled though only for a moment, I had no peace.

As sight of the distant water tower heralded our approaching destination, a sense of relief was mine, for surely she would be boarding the coach for the Temple. She did. But none could have predicted the picture she painted as she made her way towards the parked coaches. From somewhere she produced a full-length overcoat that brushed the calf-length boots and with one hand holding the umbrella high, the other towed behind her a large wheeled aircraft 'carry-on' case! One assumption was that Qena had become her home and that the boat had been a preferred mode of transport. Another was that she was going to set up a stall selling clothes alongside the other street vendors. How wrong that all proved to be. Two hours later she returned to board the boat again. The umbrella was still held high and the case was still in tow. It is said the ancient Temple had never seen anything like her before.

Crete Instead of Egypt

I am so glad we went to Crete. How different from Egypt. Knossos Palace, that most amazing archaeological site of Minoan civilisation, foremost among the large numbers of palaces unearthed on this small island, was of great interest. It was whilst reading about the excavation there, I discovered that in 1929 Arthur Evans, the virtual owner of Knossos, had appointed a certain John Pendlebury to be the curator of that archaeological site. The name seemed to ring a bell.

Was he the same Pendlebury who in late 1920s started excavating at Tell el-Amarna with the Egyptian Exploration Society and within a couple of years was promoted as director? Indeed he was. So even in Crete it seemed we could not escape Egypt. Not having been on this island previously, we wanted to see something other than the all-inclusive delights of our hotel, situated directly under the flight path of the airport. Duly we took a tour of the western half of the island, and discovered another Mediterranean gem.

In the afternoon we arrived at a place called Souda Bay where, when the situation allows, you are invited to visit the Commonwealth War Graves Commission Cemetery that is situated there. Gathered from preliminary resting places, those who gave their lives in that valiant attempt to save the island from German occupation have now been laid to rest in a delightful setting. These places are so moving for me, as I grew up to the sound of sirens, carried a gas mask to school and well knew the inside of air-raid shelters.

The life-span of so many young soldiers was very short, so it was a surprise to find a headstone referring to an age of 37 years. We had discovered the grave of John Pendlebury, the curator of Knossos. It was the third resting place of his body, following his summary execution by the German soldiers.

Apparently, unable to prove that he was not a soldier because of wounds received and having being cared for at a farmhouse, where they dressed him in local clothing, he was taken outside, leant against a wall and shot in the head and chest. This account has recently been challenged. Now the story goes that on hearing the advancing enemy troops and unwilling to bring the devastation of reprisals upon the lives of those who sought to save him, he walked out to meet his destiny. Fearing no foe, he fell as the bullets did their deadly work, whilst saving the lives of those who sheltered him.

In a recent biography called 'The Rash Adventurer', Imogen Grundon has done a great service to us all by making this young man live again in our imagination.

In his time there was great romanticism surrounding the relationship between Egypt and her neighbours. Who owed what to whom and who had borrowed what from where, could mix mythology with history and archaeology in a way that today would invite a great degree of speculation. Pendlebury dressed the part, lived the life, did the deeds and died a heroic death, beloved, and all in such a way as to invite speculation about fact and fiction.

Was his inspiration those whose life and times he sought to bring to light for ever-new generations? As he strode the countryside of Crete, through its mountains and its passes, down its precipitous cliffs and its sandy coves, being Crete to the Cretans and Spy Master to military intelligence, did he see himself as a Pharaoh or a modern day Minoan monarch?

The Beauty of Birds

In its desert setting, the fertile ribbon of land along the Nile serves as a highway for birds. Some have found a permanent home here whilst others pass through as the seasons give them license in migration. This makes for many surprises but nothing surpasses the poise and diversity of the waders, who line every metre of the banks of the Nile.

Cattle Egrets have a penchant for the trees that line the start of the road going north from Luxor to Qena, where their gregarious nature finds expression in the nesting colonies found there. The beautiful Nile Sun Bird that has made this land its own secretes itself away in the lush gardens that now abound around the large hotels, offering for self-disclosure the dull and frumpy female. Noisy Pied Kingfishers endlessly thrash their wings to stay in one place, whilst high above, Black Kites riding thermals, soar ever higher and higher without so much as a wing beat. The abundance of Squacco Heron, with their tortured necks affixed to their bodies like some gross disfigurement, stun the rapid fall of darkness with a brilliant display of white, like a signature of light, set to mark the boundaries and the banks, as they move from one watchful station to the next.

A vivid green adorning a bird in the wild is something of a surprise. Such colour would more likely be found in a cage. The only other green I have seen to match this extravagant display is the African Green Pigeon from further south, but the bird to which I here refer is the brilliant Little Bee-eater. And hovering is the pastime of another bird of grace and beauty, often found waiting on the wires, with tail gently bobbing, eyes glued to the ground. This is the Black Shouldered Kite who haunts the dusk whilst hunting.

But I have found a place where every bird can bestow an unearned beauty upon its underside. To see this magical display you have to be in a prone position, on your back, looking towards the sky. Where else could you spend long periods in that position but beside the hotel pool? The Winter Palace pool in Luxor ranks among the better pools along the Nile.

'What bird was that?' flashed through my mind as it hurried overhead. Never before had I seen such beautiful turquoise under-parts. It was not long before I realised the optical delusion or illusion, if you prefer. Every bird that flew over the brilliant blue pool could not avoid reflecting back the rich colour from below. I watched the humble sparrow's muddled browns transformed to colour matching paradise contenders. Palm Doves, for a few moments became more brilliant than their cousins and even the ubiquitous House Crow gained an azure hue. The already multi-coloured Hoopoe became a technicolour marvel. Lying there my imagination set me wondering, what other birds from home would I like to see given this makeover?

For the other extravaganzas you have to sojourn beside the Red Sea and there you are not so much spoilt but rather lost for choice.

Intoxication

At night everything seems to change. Colours, shapes and textures of the day assume new appearance after darkness has fallen. How true this is in Egypt. There seems no business during the daytime, except for tourists. The morning tries to lurch toward wakefulness but it is nearly always unsuccessful. Come the darkness then it is a different story. New sounds begin to fill the air and new activities abound. Walk through the renovated Souk in Luxor, which has a 'special' market everyday, according to the Kalesh drivers, who for five Egyptian will take you to it, albeit via a circuitous route.

Darkness births a new human dawn when all comes to life. Against it contests the light that man has made and it doesn't even compare. Manufactured noise gives way to the human voice that can be heard in all its Babel variety. However the urge to sell attempts to undo the destruction of the tower, restoring one new common language and judging by the purchases, could be deemed to be quite successful.

Youth and age mingle even to midnight and beyond but there is a lack. It does not take long to work out that it is the fair sex who are so elusive. The horse and donkey's days seem not to end at nightfall either, yet without head or tail-light they seldom seem to have an accident. Colours seem not only to invade your sight but also to attack your senses, which is born out when photographs are processed and studied back at home. There is often a dimension missing, which when present, marks out the photographer from the people who take pictures, skill.

Have you ever had that tantalising experience of having your memory evoked by a particular scent? Suddenly you are back in your childhood, in your grandmother's kitchen, in the musty library or on that first date. For the lover of exotic scents the Souk must seem like paradise. The sensitivity of the olfactory is tested to the limit. If it were a requirement to name but some of what is being experienced, few would pass a test of ten. My assumption was that intoxication required alcohol, not most readily available in shop or supermarket here. How wrong I am. Scent is intoxicating and the Souk does excel in great degree. However, after dark take a walk toward the Old Winter Palace, turn into the entrance of the New Winter Palace and continue straight ahead. Leave the air-conditioning behind as you part the glass doors and step into the garden. After dark the shrub that lines the walkways bloom with insignificant flowers but oh, the perfume! It hangs heavy on the night air and those who linger know an intoxication that haunts the senses until the addiction is again satisfied.

Tradescantia and Bougainvillea

Who could have come up with names like that? Only those who aspire to the status of scholar, I would imagine. However, these names have a beauty all their own even before you begin the quest to discover to what they have been ascribed.

The bed of Tradescantia, showing just the leaves, was a very deep purple, almost black and so it stayed contrasting with the emerald green of manicured grass for almost two weeks. White was the first of the Bougainvillea bracts to show, then came the yellow, to be later followed by the pinks, purples and vermillion. Then the Tradescantia decided it was time to flower. Set against the foliage, the nondescript petals looked as though some pink candyfloss had been caught on the wind and deposited there.

Now at home, we would struggle to get such plants to thrive in small pots and can only admire the garden centre display which provokes the purchase, only to see them wither in a day or two of exposure to central heating. I remember well the first time I saw the Bougainvillea for sale. The pot was quite small and the bracts were vibrant with colour. It was to be the winter reminder of the Mediterranean climate all through the long dark months. So it proved to be. However, the time came to repot this prized specimen and replete with good-quality potting compost and my personal addition of some used tea bags, it was soon again adorning the bay window. What took its fancy there I do not know but we became convinced that the Curse of the Triffids was visiting us.

Secateurs were needed for pruning and I will swear it grew six or so centimetres through the night. In the end it had to be discarded for it did everything except produce the bracts! That too was not as easy as it sounds for it had produced sharp thorns, which required leather gloves to be worn for handling purposes. I put it out to be removed with the rubbish but alas the bin men would not take it so it had its own solitary cortège to the tip.

Therein is the delight of visiting the lush and verdant waterside gardens of Egypt. What we can only see here in pots, there can be enjoyed in all its unconfined and rampant glory.

Did it Once Flow South?

Ancient tales, told after the consumption of a few wee drams, say the great Nile once flowed south. What a great conversation opener in the bar, on the boat or in the hotel. Taught that presentation and confidence can be used to great effect to obscure the truth, great excitement and emotion can be generated among friend and foe alike.

Sure, there was a time when no great waterway existed in the land now called Egypt but as Tectonic Plates moved and mountain ranges rose, the run-off of precipitation would have been in a more westerly rather than northerly direction. However, the day would come when the north would win but it would take many millennia. I say, 'great waterway,' for at that time its name resided, not in the mind of man, but maybe in the mind of some great ancestral being, so who knows what it might have been? Today's name Nile is derived from the Greek 'Nielos' and simply means 'River Valley.' That and the water running through it, has had other names at various times.

It is said that the ancestral Nile began as a valley called the Eonile in the Miocene Epoch, around five million years ago, when there was a warmer global climate. When the Mediterranean began to flood again after its time of desiccation, we move towards the Pliocene Epoch, spanning the interval from about 5.3 million to 2.6 million years ago and the name is changed to Paleonile, when the whole valley from Sudan to well north of Cairo became an arm of the Mediterranean Sea. Following the retreat of the sea level, a time called Pleistocene starts, the time period that spanned from 2.6 million to around 11,700 years ago, marking a dry valley phase with no water and no river. When water again began to flow, the name Prenile is encountered and from then on in to the present day, the lakes and mountains much further south in Africa began to do what Herodotus declaimed, 'gift' Egypt. Apparently the Holocene Epoch, the geological epoch which began at the end of the Pleistocene and continues to the present started that.

As children, we were taught that the River Thames once froze over in the 18th Century so that a fair was set up on the ice. Our small eyes widened and we wondered if that might happen to our small brook, The Windrush, in the Cotswolds. Imagine my surprise when I discovered that the Nile has frozen over twice in recorded history in 829 and 1010. (At least, according to Wikipedia it did. I do not need the presentation and the confidence to obscure the truth here. Computer says, 'Yes'!)

Christmas on the Corniche

Many are the ways of marking the beginning or even the end of the Muslim fast of Ramadan. Tradition prevails in Luxor as the reverberations of the fired canon echo up and down the Corniche. To be close to it, in the small park opposite the Police Station, (most of which has now been lost in redevelopment) can leave the ears ringing for hours but noticeably less if you are hungry. However, being cosseted in the numerous starred hotels could give insulation and protection.

When the Christian seasons of Advent and Christmas coincided with the Fast, strange anomalies became apparent. Tutankhamun, resplendent in his chariot, hauled by two plumed polystyrene chargers precariously balanced amidships, holding the reins, disappeared. For eleven months he graced the spacious air-conditioned entrance lobby of the Egotel Hotel and must have become one of the most photographed pieces of polystyrene in the whole of Egypt. But where, oh where did he go for that short four-week vacation that spans the end of December and the beginning of January each year?

His replacement would seem to have drawn the short straw, being hidden away for eleven months of the year, only to surface for the prescribed four-week season. Did they exchange places? Did they visit a renovator's workshop or were they simply shrouded with large dust sheets in a hidden Charnel House?

It was, of course, the replacement that caught the eye and captured the imagination. I suppose it was the first view of the lame camel that caused the questioning; certainly he looked lame with four legs of uneven length. His hump was as high as his tail was short and as far as his familiarity with the desert was concerned, it was clearly non-existent.

Shorter than the camel, yet still displaying incongruous proportions, stood several figures dressed in some form of Arab attire that defied identification. A lady and two men graced the space defined by the camel and the crib. This Nativity scene, with figures at least a metre tall, set in traditional pose, I am sure would not have impressed St Francis, the progenitor of the ritual of the crib scene, who used real people as a grand teaching aid for those who would have found it difficult to read and write. I say 'traditional' pose and that is right up to a point, for there was an angel, together with a Mary, a Joseph and a baby Jesus. What however was different, was the livestock. Gone the sheep and oxen and whatever else there might have been. Just the lonely crippled camel, looking rather the worse for wear, having been brought out from somewhere for this festive extravaganza. This attempt to make the guests from the decadent west and beyond feel at home was not only admired but also even photographed and greatly appreciated. It afforded a wonderful juxtaposition of images for the inevitable events at homecoming, when pictures captured on cameras, film and video would be shared, ad-nauseam, with friends and relatives.

The Queen of the Desert

When recalling the experience of a 'Bahariya Massage' I mentioned a meeting with Cassandra Vivienne and identified her as the 'Doyen of the Desert' and her loss of the title 'Queen of the Desert.

It happened in an unexpected and surprising way. Peter, pronounced Pietir, as he spoke with a heavy Germanic accent, was the owner of this Oasis 'hotel' with its simple rooms gathered around the central medicinal pool created by a hot spring.

He it was who greeted us, walking past all the women and making for the men. Profuse with apologies he explained that a party from Germany had recently visited and had exhausted his supply of wine. With even greater grovelling he also apologised that he had been unable to secure the services of a male masseur for a number of weeks and totally understood how devastated we would all be on hearing such news. However, there was a slight chance that one might be on his way.

Next we were invited to sign in at the 'hotel' which proved to be a daunting task as he stood between us and the receptionist behind the counter. To do as he bid us meant that we had each, one at a time, to endure a personal greeting. This involved allowing him to invade our personal space, giving his hands a great deal of freedom to roam. It involved a strong embrace followed immediately by a kiss aimed at the lips but landing on the cheek, if you had enough agility and saw what was afoot. He also tried a second time, at least giving you chance to offer the other cheek. Whilst thus engaged in such a lengthy wrestling welcome, others hurriedly headed for the welcome desk pretending to look very busy.

It was as this process was unfolding that one of the guests informed us that the veritable Queen of the Desert, none other than Cassandra Vivienne herself, was staying at the same 'hotel', which evoked a loud definitive statement from Pietir, "She iss not zee Quveen ov zee Dezert, I am zee Quveen of zee Dezert!"

Expense and Experience

There is a warning in one of the most reliable Guides to Egypt, namely The Rough Guide by the talented guide and travel writer, Dan Richardson. It concerns the Feluccas (sail boats) of Luxor. Along the Corniche, between the moored Nile Cruisers, lie small jetties around which the feluccas huddle in the often still and listless air. Like some long deceased reptiles of a bygone age, they stand tall, devoid of flesh, shivering. All that is heard is a skeletal rattling as the endless river traffic agitates the water and disturbs the rigging.

What does however draw attention is to be found high above the lapping water. Here, to walk the marble promenade is to be accosted. "Banana Island? You know how much? Only one price! Only 10 Egyptian! Maybe tomorrow?" This constant recurring chorus pursues you even in your sleep. 'La shokran', no thank you, does nothing to deter.

Had you started near the Novotel Hotel, now renamed the Iberotel and who knows what next, then walked towards the Egotel, the more observant would have noticed that the greater the distance covered, so the increasing age of those engaged in the accosting. Small boys would be replaced with those enjoying teenage years, then to be replaced by sturdier young men, until almost at your destination, should it have been the Egotel, you might by now have encountered the men of more mature years. Question and answer would have remained the same, only expense and experience would be different. Go north, the guide book tells you. It is right!

He was so charming, so persuasive and even handsome, that we agreed.... but not to Banana Island. The price agreed was neither too expensive or seemingly too cheap but as always some adjustment would be sought upon arrival, in settlement for sweet tea from Nile water well boiled on the Primus.

Hardly an obstacle course, more a forest floor littered with fallen branches, the jetty had to be negotiated, before the comparative comfort of the cushioned boat was achieved. Just how all the manoeuvres are accomplished, that sees this barque leave its peers behind and finds free water, always remains a mystery. Sure-footed as a mountain goat, the diminutive skipper leaves no square foot of surface left untrod, as with ropes and rudder in hand, often at the same time, he accomplishes that which at first seems impossible. Tacking south with the afternoon breeze giving substance to the sail, the craft glides so smoothly yet relentlessly onward. Before your senses gain control of you again, Banana Island is approaching and you just know this trip is going to cost.

"Yes, yes, we will drift with the tide and return quicker than we came," is the reassurance given in the face of anxious thoughts expressed that darkness might descend before the landing stage again came into view.

Now downstream seems to demand more difficult manoeuvres than the previous direction. Is it my fancy, or has something of his confidence deserted this young man? The activity seems hurried, the turns seem sharper and the sides of the vessel seem deceptively closer to the surface of the river.

There is no warning! The water rushes into the boat as the side dips beneath the surface. Everything on one side is immersed, from people to possessions. It feels cold and certainly touches places that it should not. The camera, fortunately, is around the neck and so avoids a baptism but the binoculars are not so lucky. Already thoughts are forming that will be the basis for debate concerning costs, should we eventually reach security without having to swim!

The young man finally regains his composure and gets us home, safely, though rather wet. When, yet again, in fading light, we begin to retrace our steps, in preparation for climbing up to the Corniche, he comes running, jumping all obstacles in his path, to claim his fare. I thrust some notes in his hand and knowing it will not be enough to satisfy his demand I keep moving on. The calls get louder and I try to explain that the portion of fare withheld is part compensation for our damp condition. He persists. It is not until we are well along the way to the hotel that he gives up. He is still calling on his father and his father's father to exact recompense from us on the morrow.

This has to be the one place where expense and experience always go together. Had I but believed the book!

The Bird Man of Aswan

His colourful calling card sets an inquisitive nature racing. 'Nile Fluka' 'Captien Sugar' 'Elphantin Island'. Would the impact be the same were it in French, German or Italian? 'El Captien' services visitors to Aswan by conducting tours in motor boats on the 'Nile First Cataract' and exciting experiences they are.

Once wild, turbulent and impassable the First Nile Cataract has been tamed by dams and the river now passes on its placid, peaceful way. In multiple perambulations, it circumnavigates the giant granite outcrops that once caused chaos but now create habitat that, for the practiced eye, contains the delights Captain Sugar will reveal.

As close as it can get, the boat is manoeuvred into place and the engine cut. The wealth of bird life on the small islands is disclosed and it soon becomes apparent which is the favourite of the Birdman. No one can say, 'striated' with such eloquence. Sometimes he can stretch the word for several seconds and if you are wondering to what bird this refers, it is of course, a Heron!

A voice from further back in the boat vocalises what many are thinking.

"Are there any crocodiles this side of the Dam?"

"Wait," is the instruction, given in muted tones. "We may or may not be lucky."

Moving across a stretch of open water towards another island, we suddenly change course. Captain Sugar had seen something we have not. The engine is cut again. As we drift toward yet another group of granite rocks, almost hidden by the tall reeds. He points to the waterline. With its crab-like gait, a crocodile is moving cautiously, making the reeds move as he goes, helping to disclose his presence. Far from being fully grown, it is only about two metres long. How long will it survive with the predatory presence of so many searching it out?

To our amazement, on visiting a larger inhabited island, the young Arab boys were eager to show us their 'pets'. In large glass aquariums were baby crocodiles ranging from 20cms to 50cms, about a dozen of them. For 'Baksheesh' we were allowed to handle them, but were left wondering from whence the eggs and where the hatching and for what purpose? Captain Sugar could keep secrets.

Desert Protection

Deep in the Sahara, not all that far from the border with Sudan, we began looking for a suitable campsite for the night. Eventually we chose a depression between two high dunes which would hopefully provide shelter from any wind that might whip up a sand storm. Always final judgement of a site is left to the drivers of the 4x4s, whose knowledge of the desert had an intimacy none of us could match.

The desert winds seem to have a language all their own and seldom is silence what we have sometimes imagined. All went well with the unpacking of the vehicles, assembling of the kitchen and dining area, and the distribution of the thin sponge mattresses which so many of us appreciated. Preference for pitches varied from those who liked to be in the lee of the vehicles, to those who could hardly put enough distance between themselves, others and the corral of vehicles; the main reason being the avoidance of those who could detain the sleep of the majority through the snores of the minority!

Only now and again was there a different sound. In the midst of all that was going on, those who did hear it didn't take any real notice. It took a while for everyone to agree to have a quiet time of listening but then discussion started. How could we be in the deep desert and hear the sound of traffic on tarmac, for that is for all the world what it sounded like? However, it was so fleeting and so infrequent and there were no roads for hundreds of kilometres. Discussion followed through the evening meal and then around the camp fire. Every so often glances were exchanged and an eerie unease settled among us as the intermittent sounds sent bristles on the neck into the vertical position. Those whose tents had been pitched a distance from the vehicles made sure they came nearer. As time to enter them for the night arrived, we watched as the lead driver moved up the gentle incline and then turned to tackle the steep gradient of the dune.

Slung across his shoulder was something we could not make out but we thought we knew he had no gun. All went very quiet and sleep overcame the company. Morning saw the mystery resolved as news was brought that within a few kilometres of our site was a brand new tarmac road cutting through the desert, unmarked on any map. From whence it started and to where it went, to this day we have no idea, for moving off in the morning it was neither seen nor heard, except by the Lead Driver who with a spade and not a gun, had sought our protection on the summit of the dune.

The Blue Blow Up

Furniture for desert travel becomes a more important topic for those of an older, more arthritic age. The softer sand, which always seems more comfortable, is never a suitable surface for anything that has four legs. Quickly you sink and slide as weight is applied and what set out as perfect equilibrium, becomes a painful new posture. There is of course, the potential of excavation, where an attempt to mould the sand to the contours of the body is undertaken. However, this is better for a prone position and can be used to great effect to watch the shooting stars, space debris, geo stationary orbiters and the great space station, not forgetting the great constellations that have captivated man from earliest days and continue so to do. The brilliance of the night sky, devoid of light pollution, provides extraordinary viewing potential when the campfire has been extinguished and the only remaining warm glow is the one inside you (evidence of a 'wee dram').

So, when I saw it in the gadget shop window, I at once recognised its potential. No possible concessions were made to desert camouflage and once inflated I did wonder if it would be visible to those in space as they are visible to us. Small in size when deflated, the box would fit precisely in the bottom of the soft holdall, that often doubled as a low level seat for supper in the desert. My mind made up, I entered the shop, and dodging various things flying around my head, I selected my purchase and took it to the discreetly tattooed lady who, by the figure and dress code, had clearly recently failed the Next New Model competition.

The box was never opened until it was unveiled in the desert. No one was watching me to begin the process, as no one was expecting anything out of the ordinary. It was when the wheezing started that folk began to look up and then to congregate. Standing there, with my mouth and face buried in a bright blue mass of plastic, all that could be heard were my vain attempts to inflate this monster. Others volunteered and in about half an hour, resplendent on the sand, sat one bright blue opaque armchair.

Alas before I had time to test its succour to my abdomen, a very gentle breeze drifted through the group, who were standing aghast at such a wondrous sight. The chair began to roll and roll. Quickly I had to recover it or else it would be disappearing across the dunes, maybe never to be seen again and cause more consternation for the lonesome Bedouins, who from time to time leave Luxor to look for the illicit to retail in the Souk.

So lesson one was quickly learned. Never leave the chair unsatupon. Lesson two was altogether something else. If the inflation had involved many willing mouths what now about deflation? I took out the plug and watched to see the air escape from this rotund masterpiece. At first it seemed that nothing was happening and indeed it wasn't. Did it have anything to do with pressure outside the shimmering sphere being equal to the pressure inside? My minimal physics suggested to me that the application of some pressure might do the trick so I sat upon the seat. To my consternation this did very little and I found that this desert convenience had turned into a monster that had to be wrestled, like a plastic alien to the very death.

After taking all their pictures (for the record) and howling with delight and laughter, I'm glad to say that many came to my rescue and helped me in the cause of deflation. The task accomplished, I was left to ponder the disposal of the beast. When, at the end of every trip we gather as a group to express our thanks to drivers, guides and cooks, we make a presentation. At the end of this particular foray into the hinterland there was an addition to the normal procedure. Hamdi, the most reliable of desert drivers, received an extra gift. And he who had witnessed all the wonders of inflation and deflation now has a blue blowup chair in pride of place in his flat in Cairo. It is unique to all of Egypt and I am told that many come from near and far to see the wonder.

The West Bank (of the River Nile)

Yes, I have visited the West Bank, the place of that horrendous tragedy at Hatshepsut's Temple, when terrorists came in from the desert and gunned down tourists. It was not long after it had happened and with the inevitable heightening of security, we did not quite know what to expect. The first surprise was as we were descending the steps from the aircraft at Luxor. Lining the path to the waiting coach were school children and a school band. They sang and played and gave all passengers a posy of flowers. Clearly they were pleased to see us. After being processed at the airport terminal we were all held back for a few moments before being allowed through the doors to access the coaches.

When we were allowed to leave there before us were more lines of children, different this time, and more flowers were distributed. It was a moving experience and a welcome to Egypt never to be forgotten. To think this had been set up around 11 pm! However, there was more. As the coach drove slowly along the roads and there was sufficient light for us to see, people were waving and appeared to be shouting. Yet perhaps the greatest surprise of all was to witness the Kalesh drivers on the Corniche clapping their hands in welcome (or relief).

In the light of the new day, everywhere you looked, there were machine gun nests made up of sand bags, manned by very young-looking soldiers eager to ask for 'baksheesh' towards the cost of new boots. By the look of the ones they were wearing, few laces and thin soles, they were sorely needed. Very few tourists were to be seen. The majority of hotels had laid off all their staff and Luxor was like a ghost town. Hurghada on the Red Sea Coast, was the same. Arriving out of the desert, dishevelled, dusty and exuding a rather pungent odour, there were no guests to shy away from us, no one in the bar to take one look at us and leave, for that was the traditional greeting we were used to on most trips. This day we drove down the length of the recent developments and saw only one pair of holidaymakers. Everywhere was deserted and it really did look again like one vast building site.

Returning to Cairo via Hurghada, waiting in the departure lounge, I overheard a conversation. "Luxor was very nice and no, we did not go to the West Bank. That is where the Palestinians live who are constantly threatening Jerusalem and we would not think of visiting them."

Coptic Conundrum

Not all realise that monasteries abound in Egypt along with churches. It does seem a little anachronistic to some, as to the lady who as we were on a coach journey around the city of Aswan exclaimed, as we passed the new Cathedral, " Oh look, they are putting crosses on the mosques now, how nice".

The vast majority of monasteries are ruins from the ancient past when virtually the whole of Egypt was Christian, before the Islamic faith arrived with the Arab invasion. They are, of course, great archaeological sites in their own right. However, there was a great revival of interest in the monastic movement from the 1970s, led by a young chemist, that saw in the ensuing years a great influx of noviciates from the ranks of intellectuals with engineers, scientists, and high-tech graduates queuing to join up. There is also a living, flourishing Coptic Church that sustains a network of churches across the land with as much as 18% of the population adhering to that faith. A visit to the Wadi Natrun where there is a concentration of ancient monasteries will be well rewarded, as rich insights will be gained into this contemporary phenomenon.

Being extremely self indulgent for a moment, I recall a wonderful side excursion to Dier Abu Mina or The Monastery of St Menas. Soldier, saint and martyr, Menas is always depicted as standing between two camels and is perhaps the most famous of all the Coptic martyrs. It was in the Roman Emperor Constantine's time that a small oratory was built over his tomb and a little later Athanasius, the early Church Father, built the first church on the site. It very quickly became a healing shrine and thousands of people from all over the Christian World visited it. The next development was its conversion into a huge basilica by a Patriarch named Theophilus. All this happened over the course of about a hundred years and by the fifth century a huge city and a royal palace had been built alongside the site. The population grew and grew. Hundreds of priests were in attendance. Around 12,000 soldiers were garrisoned near the site and then there were the city residents and those engaged in the manufacture and sale of the clay jars imprinted with 'Menas' and his two camels. In these the pilgrims carried home sacred oil for anointing the sick. Some was also used to keep the perpetual lamp alight in the sanctuary.

In 1907 excavation at the vast site began. Today it is a magnificent ruin and every phase of the ancient development can be clearly seen. For me it was one of the most evocative ancient church sites I have visited. But what astonished me was the fact that part of the railway, which the German archaeologist had constructed to transport the vast amount of coloured marble to the coast for shipment to Europe, was still in situ.

However, this is not the end. In 1961, the first stage of a new monastery close to the site was dedicated. As you approach today you see high mounded earth ramparts, hiding from view a high white wall surrounding the completed construction, which we were assured was built with money donated by the Coptic community living in the USA, numbering around 100,000. The impression that lingers in the mind is of a vast white, heavily iced cake decorated with gold embellishments. Totally out of place, it would look more at home in Disneyland.

The Father, a monk from this establishment, going by the name of Epiphanes, conducted us around the ancient site. Dressed in his flowing black robes and his tight black skullcap, embroidered with the twelve crosses, said to represent the twelve apostles, he looked the part and could have stepped from a time capsule of another age. Retuning with us on the coach that had taken us on this romantic trip, suddenly he confronted us with the reality of the present day. From somewhere beneath the voluminous folds of his black habit, the melodious tones of a cell phone were heard to ring out as he wrestled with his garments to silence the offence. From the rest of us peels of laughter, in which he heartily joined in, rang round the vehicle.

We shouldn't have been so surprised, for on reflection, the great white iced cake was laden with aerials, satellite dishes, and microwave masts.

Mattresses and Moods

To whom is given the wisdom to know what lures a human being to the desert? From the Egyptian perspective it began with gold I imagine, which continues to this day. In later Christian days it was compounded by a flight from the persecutions of the church with the power struggles of the Bishops, to gain and maintain the ascendency to power that drove many to embrace the desert. With the advent of the Emperor Diocletian's systematic persecution, which focused on amendment of beliefs or termination of life, a new exodus to the desert places began to gather pace. This is how Monasticism began, as Christians seeking solitude and minimal distraction, felt attracted to the solitude. The desert provided the ideal situate for exposure to privation and the enhancing of self-discipline. Mainly young men, who gained inspiration from the examples in Jesus' ministry, where he sought solitude and his precursor, John the Baptist, who cut his teeth in the isolation of the desert, sought a new experience where the world could be left behind and God's call lived out in an innovative way, which almost appears to be incarnation in reverse, following a God who breaks into the world and provoking followers to flee from it. (Please excuse my theological musings.)

Those of us who venture into the desert in comfortable 4x4s seem not to be troubled by such high and lofty motivations, or so I thought. We were not escaping anything. On the contrary, we were seeking something. However, there were times when it seemed we were not all seeking the same thing and certainly not all in the same way. I should have guessed that this would be a different trip when a woman hit me.

We were in the public bar at the team briefing on the night before we began our journey into the desert. Her husband chided her, telling her that I might not agree with all her ideas but to be patient and await the desert. It all had to do with some theories that had invaded her mind and apparently the desert would be the place of resolution. Interesting motivation I thought. Most of us went armed with logbooks, pencils, tape measures, the odd GPS and the like. Our task, to locate, record, describe and measure more of the rock art of the Eastern Desert which the likes of Winkler, Wiegell, Mons and a few others had recorded almost a century before. She, I was to discover, went seeking something else.

The wadi was wide and through the blurred haze of the distance, gently coloured pastel shades of pinks and greens could be observed. Here we had seen gazelle and as a consequence were always scanning where the rocks and sand meet, for the tell-tale wisps of dust that disclose their movements.

The campsite chosen, the drivers began to throw down the mattresses, which added that touch of relief for those of us whose backs were beginning to make concessions to the years. Remembering which you had used previously was often a test complicated by the amount of liquid consumed the night before. Looking around I saw, some distance from the rest, two tents being erected. They too would be in need of mattresses, so gallantly I shouldered some and made my way towards their chosen spot. Putting them down outside the tents, I called to say what I had done. In a few moments the occupants emerged and began to inspect the said mattresses. To my surprise I was told that they were the wrong colour and would I change them please?

"Is there a preferred colour?" was my next question.

"Mauve, because today is a mauve wadi day and the

mood is also mauve and we have seen the rock carved boats that are going to be found tomorrow," was her explanation.

Now I was learning fast and remembered the incident in the Bar. There she had been telling me about her visit beneath the second Sphinx and it had been disclosed to her a cancer cure was available. She had had the formula made up and tested and it worked. Credulity forbids me to go further but I began to understand a little more why they had sought the desert.

Ballet in the Desert

A tent can be such a convivial home in the desert. However, there have been those who, from time to time, have been known to discard it, as they sought a night open to the sky and stars. My difficulty has always been to get from the horizontal to the vertical. So as not to tempt fate too much at dawn, I would undo the tent zip and slide myself, still flat, out of the tent. So the first thing I would see would be the sky and any clouds there might be. Then with a rolling motion turn, tummy down and survey the sand from ground level. Sometimes others beat me to it and having escaped their tent were about their ablutions, not too far away. I think the activity is called 'mooning'. The Brown Necked Ravens are always up before us and busy themselves clearing any remnants of food we may have left from the night before. Chiff Chaffs will settle on your shoes and even binoculars, resting from the rigours of migration. Residents like the White Crowned Black Wheatear never seem to be far away. But one puzzle is the presence of dragonflies!

However, on this particular morning it was none of these attractions that caught my attention, rather an apparition some way off across the desert sand. Yes, I did rub my eyes and wonder if I was awake or whether this was part of a dream sequence. There she stood, resplendent in her leotard in a rather exotic pose. Stationary but for a moment, she began the daily ritual that every ballet dancer has of necessity to engage in, in order to continue to function freely in that profession over the years. Against the backdrop of the green and red glow of the sand that is found in this particular place, there was an ethereal quality about what I was observing.

Unsteadily I stood up in my garments of the night and looked around. Sentinel-like, standing beside each small tent, were almost all the occupants and all eyes were fixed, where moments before mine had been, marvelling at this spectacle. There was an anticipatory moment when I thought that some notes of music, that might already have been playing and which as yet, I could not hear, would come drifting up the shallow depression that marked our camp site. It all looked so painful, yet at the same time so precise and from one whose years would not have led you to believe that such was possible. There was a pause and as in the concert hall, uncertain if the end had really come, a gentle ripple of applause was heard to echo down the smoothness of the sand.

The Pregnant Camel

Careful observation of the desert floor can tell many a tale. The abundance of the remains of the fruit of the Higlig tree lying beneath, tells of the number of camels that have passed that way. Under the Acacia tree, sharp needles that can penetrate the thickest of soles, bid the walker beware and the sitter not to sit. Around the base of the sporadic tree, tiny almost imperceptible tracks disclose the presence of ants. Woe betide the one who leans against that trunk, for later irritation can give way to injection of formic acid and good as that can be for the system, the puncture point can give rise to considerable inflammation or infection.

Flint, flint flakes, flint tools, scrapers, knives and pottery fragments, all have a story to tell and it is so instructional to read the works of those who study these things, to see the wealth of information they disclose. Grinding stones and their trays lie in abundance in some places. It is there I like to pause and let my imagination loose. I see a woman of indeterminate age, kneeling on the ground, rolling that stone backwards and forwards, grinding the grain to make flour, to mix the dough, to bake the bread, to welcome home the hunter husband weighed down with gazelle. How long ago she lived is a question I would love to have answered. Other things are there that, because of my limited knowledge, I leave untouched for another's keener eye and learning to expose. The gathered stones denoting burial and the carefully constructed ones, low now because of the weathering of the centuries, that once formed protection from the elements, have so much information to yield up.

The wells, identified through the ages, now marked out by the Bedouin sign of rope and bucket, go deep, sometimes many depths of man. And should you be as lucky as we were, in Wadi Midric, to trace its seventeen tortuous kilometres their full length, just after rain, you could see, albeit infrequently, in the still and shimmering surface of well water, your mirrored reflection. Gaze deeper still and you could be forgiven for thinking that in such clarity your soul might be exposed.

Tracks give up their evidence and tell of critters that one never sees, or seldom. The desert fox has been sighted but only on rare occasions, but regularly the spoor is seen. It is the little creatures, like the scorpion and various insect forms, that leave such trails you would think yourself in danger had you no regard to size. Snakes leave beautiful and intricate patterns as they slither from rock to rock and often a trail will disappear where they have taken to a rock to belie their presence, much as mammals use water to disguise their scent.

Droppings also tell a story. The presence of the Hyrax is more explained by its mess than its deposits. Leaving huge stains cascading down the rocks, it is one of the worst polluters of Rock Art, but that is to digress. The small precise pellets of the gazelle suggest an abundance that outweighs the sightings. Yet when seen, their grace, beauty, and speed is enchanting. Sad that those with guns invade the desert at weekends for 'sport.' The major landmark in the dropping scale has of course to be the camel. From white denoting age, to black denoting freshness, the evidence of their passing is everywhere.

A good morning's work had been accomplished, many Rock Art Sites recorded and with afternoon anticipation high we paused for one of those special salads which are the fame of our desert drivers. For once we were well grouped, as so often we would be scattered, searching shade. Most had finished lunch and were enjoying tea and would have enjoyed coffee, had it not been hidden!

Reaching down I picked up a dry camel turd. It was on the whiter end of the scale and I began to read the runes. First I rolled it around between the thumb and forefinger of my right hand, much as the connoisseur does with his expensive cigar. Then I held it to my ear, again in imitation and I'm sure that someone thought that I might be going to light it. I then began my little discourse.

"This one passed here about three months ago", I said. "She was well-grown for her age and part of a small group," I continued. "About three to four months pregnant I believe." That was the moment of interruption for which I had been waiting.

"I guess you can tell it's female but how do you know she was pregnant?" a voice with a strong American accent, carried over from behind me.

The Mad Miners

Coming across other human forms within the desert has all the potential for an adventure. Desert hospitality has always been a thing of renown where greeting, together with the exchange of some gift, is almost compulsory. All travellers in the desert are there for a reason, all have a purpose and it is not always wise for you to know the purpose of another. Indeed there are times when ignorance is a state to cherish.

Things that move in the desert create small clouds of dust and this is often what is seen in the far distance. That was the case in our first encounter. Looking through the dusty windscreen did not help with identification and distance certainly confused. First it was a tree but why the dust? Then it was one or more camels. The concluding supposition was a train! You can quickly see what state the occupants of our vehicle were in. What was eventually confirmed with a nearness that gave certainty, was that we had come across a man leading a donkey, pulling a cart. Yes, we all were wondering too, just what was he doing here? The rules of the desert demanded that we stop, exchange pleasantries, offer something in the way of food or drink, but not ask any questions. He stood at the donkey's head holding the harness and was but a few inches taller. Accepting the offer of some sweets he began to talk and our drivers later related the circumstance of his being two days walking distance from Luxor and still going away!

At that particular season of the year, in a certain wadi there grows a herb that commands a good price in the souk in Luxor. It is about three and a half days distant. The donkey has had a drink on leaving, a drink on arrival at the destination, then a drink when it gets the master safely home. On the other hand human needs demand a greater frequency of liquid consumption. That turned out to be a drink a day. For sleeping? Lie down with the donkey, having the flat-bedded cart set against any prevailing wind. Food was not mentioned. The galabeya was well worn and in vain we looked for shoes. Bare foot would be the order of the day until the lights of Luxor welcomed the returning merchant. It was all over in a very short space of time. We left him in a pall of dust created by our spinning wheels. He went on his solitary way and we were left to wonder how we could mistake a man and donkey for a train.

Now to come to the miners. We think that it was only about once a month that a wagon came to collect the spoils, bringing with it the next month's nourishment. We wondered too what could possibly be preserved from one month's end until the next that would be at all edible, let alone palatable. Looking at the two specimens that approached us, we did get the idea that they had not eaten in a long time. To call their clothes rags would be to do them an injustice and the colour of their skin did not allow us to distinguish dirt from sun-burnt black. Looking into their eyes proved very difficult for they appeared to focus everywhere but the direction of their gaze. What they were mining we did not ask and were not told, neither was it disclosed how many more were hidden in the dark recess into which we could not see. Detained a little longer than with the donkey cart and having given some stale bread that seems to be a desert delicacy, we moved away. Going on a little distance we signalled to the ladies it was now safe for them to come out from underneath their covering. We were glad that none had disembarked whilst we were stationary. All had heeded the driver's request that they stay hidden, because miners don't get to see women for very long stretches of time. We felt we had managed to avoid an international incident that could have carried some lurid headlines in certain Sunday Papers. 'British Women Captured by Sex Mad Miners'

Ahmed, Egyptian Pugilist

Over time we got to know most desert drivers well but there were the occasions when the size of our party demanded extra vehicles, which came with their owners driving or for some reason a substitute driver had to be found. The rookie was usually put at the back of the convoy under careful instructions to maintain the correct distance at all times and in all circumstances. Such was the case on this particular day. We got off to a reasonable start out of the Cairo traffic and headed for the desert highways. Once on our own, the vehicles in front began to pull further and further ahead. No real cause for concern there, as they stopped up ahead to view various rock formations and we caught them up. The next time they stopped was at one of the desert Service Stations which are of course, nothing like the ones on our own motorway network. These are in a class of their own. The tentacles of Health and Safety, Hygiene Legislation and Employment Law have not reached this far. With a sealed carton or a can you are reasonably safe but all the exciting items and delicacies are open to flies and heat. Neither is tea nor coffee what you thought it was when you left home but it doesn't take long to understand new definitions.

Clearly words had been exchanged among the drivers as moving off we found ourselves, not at the rear, where we had started out but this time in the middle of the convoy. Yet again it was not long before the vehicles in front were disappearing into the distance and those behind us were coming very close, sounding horns and generally trying to hurry us along. The next recourse to find a solution to this dilemma was to be placed at the rear of the convoy yet again but this time with a driver change. The thinking behind this was that the fault might lie with the vehicle rather than the driver. No such problem was revealed there, except that now it was another vehicle struggling to keep up. At the next stop we saw the wayward driver taken to one side being given, what seemed like quite a severe reprimand. Setting out again we took up station, again at the rear.

Being my turn to take the front seat for this leg of the journey, I decided to see if I could engage the man, we now knew to be another Ahmed, in conversation. The forthcoming response was only a series of grunts in response to both my English and my very limited Arabic. Then a new dimension to the problem emerged. We were not always able to keep all four wheels on the tarmac on some of the broad bends in the desert road that fortunately was bereft of other traffic. From time to time we strayed to the hard shoulder! Now my attention changed from conversation to eyes, his eyes. Not only in my vehicle at home but also on my motorcycle, I had experienced the sensation of drowsiness. It seemed to me that Ahmed was very tired and so it proved. Every now and then his eyes would shut. Clearly this called for some serious action if we were to arrive at our destination. With the rest of the convoy way out in the distance a three-pronged approach was adopted. To begin with I began to whistle and sing and encouraged the rest of the passengers to do the same. The results were somewhat limited. The second tactic I adopted was to try to cause him some discomfort as I poked him in the ribs. This too did not accomplish all we would have liked. However, the third measure was much more effective. Leaning across, I put one hand on the wheel, and in that way began to share the steering. Ahmed looked up, smiled, and made no effort to remove my hand indeed his face seemed to say he was glad it was there.

Later we got to learn a little of his story from the other drivers, who had difficulty containing their laughter. Apparently, Ahmed was quite a well-known Egyptian heavy weight boxer who had the unenviable reputation of losing the majority of his bouts. Indeed they said, he was something of a punch bag and that could well have explained why my digging him in the ribs was ineffective. Besides that, his days in that profession were coming to an end, luckily for him, as he was having difficulty staying awake for extended periods and concentration was deserting him. A new greeting emerged between the drivers and punters after that. We would put our hands together, rest our head upon them in feigned sleep declaring, "Ahmed sleepeth."

Due to the marvels of satellite phones, the next day a new driver took up station in our 4x4 and to this day we have never seen the sleepy Ahmed again.

The Antiquities Inspector

Rules are rules are rules wherever you are and to be able to visit what you want to visit in Egypt, it pays to abide by the letter. That is what we do. However, the rules do not only have an impact on the visitor but also on our Egyptian colleagues. However should it be the Fast of Ramadan, then that will overrule everything.

All the passports and visas were correct. All passes to all destinations were in order. There did however, remain a new regulation for vehicles but that was also addressed. It was Ramadan. This meant that no one would be available to check all that paperwork until after sunset. We ensconced ourselves outside army HQ gates, on the roadside verge. Every half hour we sent someone different to try to gain admission, whose assignment, once inside the walled compound, was to try to get to the Officer in Charge. The afternoon wore on. Darkness began to fall. Sunset came and went. Roadside vendors offered to share their Break-Fast with us. Still no sign or word. The clock continued ticking. We had a long way to go before we could camp in the desert that night.

Then at last the big black gate swung back and from the wide exposed space, what seemed to be a diminutive figure emerged waving a piece of paper. The big black gate swung back again into its place and the cry went up for all to board the vehicles before someone changed their mind. One further task remained before we could climb to the main road and set our sights for the tasks ahead. It all had to do with some new regulation that decreed that our foray into the desert had to be in the company of one of the local antiquities inspectors.

Ah, poor luckless man, being picked up late at night, being whisked off into the desert to spend some days and nights, and in Ramadan at that. Leaving his wife and children behind, all the boyhood stories of the desert came flooding back to him. This dangerous place of dark forces where the Jinns are supposed to live. Scared? He tried his best not to show it but as he climbed aboard he was visibly shaking.

We drove east towards the Red Sea until we came to a familiar part of the desert road, turned left across the sand, and doubled back upon ourselves. The vehicles formed an arc, turned on the headlights to give us some light and we began to erect our tents. By now this had become a five minute exercise for most but alas, not for our antiquity guest.

Unfortunately he had never put a tent up in his life, let alone spent a night in one. The drivers, always so willing to help us, seemed strangely reluctant to assist him. In headlight brightness, he stood. Holding his bale aloft, that hardly resembled a tent, with the brightness of his eyes clearly picked out in the surrounding darkness by the lights, he looked lost. He was still visibly shaking. We had pity on him. Starting to erect his tent we discovered that clearly something was wrong. With many gesticulations we discovered that he wanted it put as close the vehicles as possible, while most of us preferred some distance. When we had finished you could not squeeze between the 4x4 wheel arch and the tent entrance. When up, we put his overnight bag inside, however, just what it contained we never did discover, indeed it was very small. Too late for supper, having shared the sunset feast some hours ago, we now retired to our tents ready for an early morning start.

The morning brought the anticipated expectation for all save one, whose morning demeanour suggested that he had not slept, even for a moment. How would he ever manage four more nights in the deep desert? Would he ever see his wife and family again and on return would he terminate his employment and forever seek city safety?

Five days later we dropped him off outside his house. There was such a commotion as his wife and boys ran to embrace him. Never again would he say yes, when a volunteer was needed.

Navy on the Nile

I had heard of the Battle of the Nile, August 1st and 2nd 1798, when Admiral Nelson achieved that amazing naval victory, but by the Nile? For the Nile? On the Nile? I did not know! Why is the Mediterranean not mentioned? Later, of course I read more and came across Abu Qir. But what brought all that to mind as I was standing on the top deck of the Nile cruiser, The Royal Rhapsody?

All the way from Luxor to Sohag a little inflatable had been buzzing around our Nile cruiser like a busy bee. It looked a little low in the water and then I noticed its armament, a little over the top for so frail a craft! I discovered there was a similar gun mounted on our vessel and was told that it was to inspire confidence. Did they realise it had the opposite effect? Waking early at Sohag, for we had planned visits to the White and Red Monasteries, I climbed the stairs to the top deck just in time to hear, what I presumed to be the command to 'Fall In', judging by the response on shore. Emerging from various locations a group of about 30 men, in various stages of undress, began to assemble in three irregular lines. Memories of National Service came flooding back and I know that the Royal Air Force, never renowned for its smart uniforms, only smart hairstyles, would never have dared appear in daylight looking like that. Who were these people? For a while I was quite puzzled until I realised this was the Navy. How delightful to have a Navy on a river.

Dark blue battle-dress was in disarray but as the lines were formed, trousers were pulled up, belts were fastened, buttons were secured and hats worn at a variety of angles tended to fall off when wearers bent down to tie boot laces. There appeared to be some sort of seniority, judging by the coloured flashes worn by some and others by their position in the ranks. Conversation, which I thought would be forbidden in the ranks, seemed to abound as it appeared no order to, 'Right Dress', had been given. Was this their 'Senior Service'? It had to be if their DNA went back to the Pharaonic times. It wasn't organised and sloppy would be too kind an adjective. The word rabble could have been applied. But all was to suddenly change.

A command was heard, though its meaning I did not catch and these Sohag Sailors began to shuffle into more regular lines, though still lacking any form of finesse. The command came from one who had insignia that I did not understand. He had not been too visible from where I stood but clearly he was in charge. A command for 'Attention' must have been given, for there was a general stirring in the ranks as feet were reluctantly brought more adjacent. Then he appeared, the one for whom this parade was being prepared for inspection. Walking forward, he adjusted his trousers and secured his belt, straightened his jacket, and put his cap upon his head, which also fell off when he bent to tie his laces.

Youthful Soldier

To us it seemed an unscheduled and unnecessary stop but to those who knew better, it was essential. 'Security' is a word that enables anyone to get away with everything. 'Security' is a word that legitimises the absurd. 'Security' is a word that carries the authority of the ancient gods! No one could have imagined the delights and benefits that this 'security' stop would bring to light over the next couple of weeks.

For the majority of our party the desert was calling. It had taken several days to arrive at this point. Behind us was the last outpost of the oasis and before us was the trackless expanse of near virgin sand with little or nothing to interrupt our journey all the way to the deep south west of Egypt, even to Jebel Uweinat. However, beside us was an Oasis Army Outpost. He was young, handsome, slender and smart, which cannot be said about every soldier we have met. We were here to take him on board and to regard him as our 'security' for the adventure that lay before us. Little notice was taken of him as he hurried towards the 4x4s with his 'weekend' bag hardly large enough to hold a change of clothes.

Quickly now we were under way, anxious as ever to ensure the success of this trip. After many hours of driving, the site for our first night's camp was chosen and tents were quickly erected before the light failed. It was not long before dinner was ready to be consumed, against a magnificent backdrop of stars, which because of the absence of light pollution, seemed to display just for our personal and particular delight, curtain after curtain of cosmic radiance.

Wandering around with my video camera in hand, looking for the odd, interesting shot that would stir the memory in the days to come, I spied the soldier, sitting on a mat on the sand, leaning against one of the vehicle wheels all alone. He was busily engaged in eating his dinner whilst trying to avoid any spillage from the plentiful portion of delicious gravy that might fall and discolour his uniform. As I raised the camera to see if there was sufficient light for a short clip, he became very agitated and with simple gestures, indicated that were I to proceed, he would have no alternative but to put a pair of handcuffs on me. Smiling, I turned aside, giving no indication that he was already in the 'can' and as I moved away I thought to myself that if that were the case, then by the end of the trip we would all be in handcuffs.

Just which of the ladies began to take special notice of our soldier first will never be known but it quickly became apparent that out of the eight travellers subscribing to that definition, the majority greeted him with familiar smiles, nods and winks and it was not long before the rest joined in. His initial embarrassment of blushes and nervous smiles was obvious for all to see but then he began to relax and enter into the spirit of all that was going on. Soon he was not only helping the drivers but beginning to help the paying guests too. He turned his hand to cooking, wheel changing, tent erecting and fire lighting, as well as providing for our security in a most inconspicuous way. A proportion of the ladies, some old enough to know better, wanted to borrow the soldier and I thought of the novel by Christopher Isherwood, 'May we borrow your Husband,' and was glad that thought got no further.

His change of clothes was civilian wear and he began to blend with all the excitement of the trip, insofar as when it came time for the obligatory 'group photo', the ladies insisted they be photographed with him alone. Remembering the threat to use handcuffs when I wanted to take his picture, I wondered just how many of the ladies would like him to make the same threat to them.

Desert Intoxication

Wrapping the potatoes in aluminium foil and burying them in the hot sand that framed the depression of the desert floor fire, resulted an hour or so later, in a tasty treat that supplemented the green bread and the plastic cheese. When only wood ash remains after flames and red embers are reduced to white powder, deceptive heat remains invisible. He discovered it quite by accident. What particular brand or for that matter blend of spirits he had been imbibing, none of us knew, for there was something secretive about his silent singular journeys to his tent.

No such silence pertained as he returned to companions remaining in huddles around the dying embers. The volume was, of course, adjusted by the level of alcohol intake which in turn increased after every returning visit he made. Stepping into the circle of his companions with his back to what used to be the fire, he proceeded to address the company in stentorian tones of long-ignored commands. Such was the presentation that his body became involved with the activities of his mouth. He shook from head to toe. It was at this point that his legs seemed to join in something entirely different. Alas they could not give the required support any longer. He might have fallen forward but such was the sensation of gravity under the control of inebriation, somewhat akin to toast always falling butter-side down, backwards he fell.

A startled look overtook his face. His body, gaining new momentum from some deep recess of long forgotten inertia, seemed to move almost vertically. That being a physical impossibility, some other hidden explanation must be sought. Nevertheless from the prone to the upright seemed to take only a micro-second. Many accompanying expletives followed but they seemed a mere after-thought judging by the look of surprise upon his face. Through the light layer of white ash, he had penetrated to the black as his hands and face testified. Little severe harm had been done to the flesh, but the ego had been scorched.

Who's Been Sleeping in my Bed?

The loud confrontation had all the officious intent of Father Bear when with heavy accusatory tones, he demanded, "And who's been sleeping in my bed?" The sound was heard 500 metres away but the words could not be clearly distinguished at that distance.

It began after supper, yet another wonderful meal conjured up from what remained after six nights already spent in the desert, by the multi-skilled and talented desert drivers who were, as always anxious to get home to see their families on the morrow. They too had chosen the site where, should flash floods invade the valley, they would pass us by, and the surrounding cliffs would give a modicum of protection from the wind. A couple of hundred metres wide at the mouth, with the bluffs exceeding a hundred metres in height on either side, the far end of this rocky ravine gently rose with stepped dunes enabling the easiest of access to the highest point, which in turn gave way to panoramic views across the canyon as it disclosed the full extent of the wadi stretching away into the desert. A magical place of beauty, hushed in its stillness, vibrant in its constantly changing colours, and evocative of the romance beloved of many writers.

Arrival had been in late afternoon light, casting long shadows across the desert floor but enabling all to pitch their tents in reasonable comfort as well as to see what they were doing. Multi-coloured, one, two, and even three person tents, spread out around the bright white corralled 4x4s, protected with their kaleidoscopic coloured awnings.

Each canvas or plastic shelter held one or two or three tired occupants, some diary writing, some sleeping, some chatting, some embracing, at least one iPod listening, and yet another briefly reviewing the video footage of the day but all sensing a little sadness that yet another adventure was nearly at an end.

The call to supper pierced the silence of the blackness that had crept upon us unnoticed. The pin-prick lights of various torches, penetrating the darkness with varying degrees of success, danced across the wide expanse, where they began to coalesce around the sole light bulb suspended above the vehicles casting strange shadows across the 4x4s and making them appear as monsters.

After initial chatter, quietness descended as mouths gave way to eating rather than speaking. Soon the tea and coffee were served and this was followed by a production of bottles containing such remnants from the previous week that had not yet been consumed. Some held more than others, yet however many remained, all would be consumed before the mattresses again welcomed tired bodies.

Once more conversation picked up and became animated as the alcohol went about its task of tongue loosening. A few more hours passed and small clusters of folk went their different ways. Some heard the call, 'To your tents O Israel', whilst others had the heavens to contemplate and still others allowed the darkness to embrace them as they embraced each other.

The moon is still shadow-bound as the sun continues its eternal circumnavigation, though stationary to a revolving earth, not yet having the power to dim the curtain of the stars, planets, satellites or space stations. Neither does it have the power to shed enough light across earth's surface to give form and substance to the widening wadi. From their vantage point on the higher dunes a small group of friends watch the dancing light below as it moves with a great degree of uncertainty and instability around the homestead of the last desert night.

It is from an unsteady hand that the shaking beam emits its light, for he had more spirit left than most and decided to consume it all himself. Now devoid of any sense of direction or cohesion of brain or body, and having lost the ability to walk with grace upon soft sand, he lurches from left to right, falls frequently but seeks no help or advice. Down the gentle slope and into the wider wadi is his destination. Often words of encouragement echo out to him to turn and retrace his steps, and to find rest; all to no avail. One thing remains. Go after him. I do.

It was with only the most gentle of physical pressure that I wheeled him around. I knew which way he now faced but he had not a clue. Taking some of his weight to avoid the frequent stumbles converting into falls, we made an agitated way towards the tented area. "That's my tent!" he declared with a strong but confused conviction. Before I realised what was happening, he pulled at the flap and zip.

"What are you doing in our tent?" was the cry that echoed round and certainly would have awaked all who might have drifted to the land of dreams. Protestation loud and clear came from deep within as two maidens tried to assess their chances of escape.

Struggling with more diversion therapy, I looked in vain through the darkness but could not determine which tent was his. He continued to protest that someone was sleeping in his tent. More verbal abuse to the torch, which would not point in the right direction, to the sand that was flying everywhere and to this seeming stranger hanging on to him as best he could, followed. I had a strong temptation to bury him in the cooling sand just where he fell but that would not have done my reputation much good.

The sole occupant of another tent was later surprised to discover him as a visitor. Extricating both from a very delicate situation and assuring the worried lady that he would not return, at least that night, eventually we reached a tent which I now know was his. Unzipping the flap and pushing him in, his final words paralysed me. "You will stay with me until morning after all your trouble, wont you?" Declining the invitation, I moved away to my own tent only to realise that his tent was identical to the one he had first tried to enter. So he was almost right after all.

From Where do These People Come?

Inevitably the Air Egypt flight is late. That is a guarantee in which you can have total confidence. But lateness is a relative term. Watching the route map on the seat-back video, as is my wont, we crossed the Mediterranean heading for the Egyptian coast and then hopefully, on south towards Luxor. However, on this occasion we would be really late. Instead of continuing to fly south, we began to bear left, which could only set a course parallel with the coastline. I waited for an announcement. When it came it confirmed my fear, that we were heading for Cairo and not Luxor.

The problem at Luxor was a sand storm, so it would be overnight at a hotel near to Cairo Airport, an early rise next morning, then down to Luxor. Everyone was very tired and some a little fractious when we finally arrived at the right destination of Luxor Airport early the next morning. When all the formalities were over things began to change. Some, laden with bags that should have been banned as 'carry on', others with virtually nothing, made their way to the numbered coaches to take us to the boat. Finding the right one, it was quickly filled and looking around I began to be aware of some of our travelling companions. It was a full coach to take us to the vessel for a cruise down the Nile. Ensuring that the cases had all been identified and leaving them to be carried by the crew to our cabins, we made our way along the Corniche until we found the steps leading down to the gangplank for the boat. The conversation from behind drifted forward as we descended. "You know dear, I always thought the Red Sea was wider than this!"

Notice of Arrival

One week is never enough time to do any kind of justice to the Egypt of the ancients. Those who dive among the Red Sea coastal resorts tell that a week is fine, though two are better. The Egyptophile however, has to linger. It is in the blood. Homecoming is not too strong a word to describe the emotion as the heat hits the face after the aircraft door is opened. Then the scent of horses assails the nostrils and everywhere is the experience of cigarette smoke that is beginning to vanish from the life experience at home.

There is something special about boarding a Nile Cruiser. It has a magic all its own, be it the giants of the river with more than fifty cabins, to the smaller variety with a mere twenty or so. Having sampled most, the smaller is the better as far as I am concerned and my dream is a dahabiya, that twin masted sailboat used by the earliest explorers. Aboard this floating hotel you dream you will sail for eternity. Did not the ancients build homes for eternity? Were they not the most successful nation on earth in accomplishing this?

The static hotel offers something quite different. Here the scenery does not change, familiarity with staff is not quite so intense, the distances to walk are greater but the pool is bigger. Potted shrubs give way to gardens of delight and sometimes it is hard to avoid the evening entertainment. The quality of service is consistent on boat and land, as is the lavish attention in which you are cocooned.

The major difference between the two is that for the boat,

you all arrive together but for the hotel no one knows how short or how long is your stay. I love to wonder how long a guest has been around and have discovered there are several ways to make such a deduction.

At first I was drawn to the idea that you could tell how long a person had been in residence by the body shade. Exposure to the sun, though discouraged by the medical profession, still remains a passion for the majority. Yet knowing what you can pay for these days, it is possible to deceive, both with the contents of a bottle or the time spent under a lamp. Recently, without really giving it any thought, I stumbled upon a method of deduction that was quite new to me.

In the 'duty free' of the airport I had whiled away some time. Looking through the books I spotted the latest novel of John Le Carre. A fan of his writing for many years, I snapped it up and thought it might last two days or maybe three at the most, because I, for one can never put him down. In the bag that accompanies all to the poolside, the books have pride of place. The lounger is adjusted, the tea is ordered, the sun lotion is applied, and then the choice is book or ipod or both. For me the book invariably wins. So it was that opening it and reading just a few pages I turned around and there were three or four other guests, all at about the same place in their novels. It was then I realised that I had stumbled upon a more accurate way to deduce how long a guest had been around, how many pages of the novel were left. But things move on and Kindle has destroyed my guide.

Airport Security

"Step over here, please sir? Empty your bag on this table."

In no time at all my 'carry on' was emptied and its contents exposed for all to see. That however, was not sufficient. The video had film and battery removed, the still camera had battery and card taken out. Everything that could be reduced to something smaller was taken apart and emptied. Next the officer put on latex gloves and the thought crossed my mind that such delicate examinations would usually be conducted with a modicum of privacy. I need not have feared. Some cotton wool, held securely in tweezers, was dipped in a fluid and then everything was wiped. This was then tested to see if there was any contamination with explosives. Pleased to be given the all clear, I took my time in reassembly and repacking. Inquiring why I was picked on, and at the same time, complementing the officer for the thoroughness of the operation, and glad it was done for the public's travelling safety, he had a simple reply. "You were number twenty seven." I made a mental note that I should always try to avoid being number twenty seven in future and then began to marvel at the impossibility, because I would never know where they started. This was Heathrow, not Egypt.

Being a regular traveller to Egypt meant that I never bothered much about currency. Any leftovers would always be useful on the next trip. I guess there are limits to what you can and can't take in or out but I would never ever come near those boundaries. No, it's not the amount that concerns the traveller so much as the condition. I have one

97

prized possession and it is an Egyptian one-pound note, that when it was accidentally torn in two, was so dirty that the sticky tape would not adhere, so it is stapled together with three metal staples! But the smell, how it lingers on hands and clothes.

I had seen it happen at airports shown on the television. Those trying by various means to hide drugs get accosted by sniffer dogs just nuzzling up to their legs. 'Be sure your sins will find you out', was one of my mother's two favourite sayings. The other one had something to do with clean underwear. 'Nothing to declare' was beckoning me amidst the crowd, so at first I did not notice. Then the rubbing against my legs became persistent and looking down I saw the sniffer dog. As I looked up the crowd around me melted away. It was then I saw that the dog was on a very long lead and at the other end was a man in a uniform.

"I expect its only money," his voice boomed through the hall, "check him out, will you?"

Before I could move a woman was standing beside me. I emptied my pockets and produced my remaining Egyptian currency and coins.

"Oh, that's what it is," she said, and told me to continue.

Today it's different. When all is placed at the mouth of the X-ray scanner and you are divested of your jacket, bag, belt, keys, shoes, and mobile phone, the walk of revelation stands before you. "Shall I set the alarm off this time?" is always a question in my head. On the other side of the walk-through metal detector stood, what appeared to be two Egyptian businessmen, both busily engaged in dressing after their ordeal was over. Looking my way and I thought mentally willing me to set the alarm off, I had an idea. Standing on my left leg, I waved my right one through the apparatus. Lights flashed, bells sounded and a uniformed man came running past the businessmen, who were by now falling about laughing. My knee replacement has given me notoriety at last.

Arriving in the Dark is Always Deceptive

Egypt Air offers a great travelling experience and comes highly recommended. Its daily 14.00hrs departure time from Heathrow is invariably missed and sometimes hours can pass whilst awaiting the call to board. Being fed is also an interesting experience. The call goes out, 'Meat or Fish!' And sometimes served, is cake! It is rather on the dry side and reminds me of the wartime Slab Cake, as it was called, supposedly adulterated with fine sawdust, due to the shortage of flour.

Imagine the surprise, when once boarding an internal flight in Libya, as the sign declared the time to fasten the seat belt, looking down, the Falcon Horus motif of Air Egypt was looking up. What price did the Libyans pay for the ageing Air Egypt fleet? But this is all really a diversion. What I had intended to discuss, and still intend to, is arrival after dark.

Leaving in the brightest of sunshine or the heaviest of downpours makes no difference to the speed of nightfall on the flight south. Last to be seen are the snow-capped Alps and as sleep begins to overtake the eyes, daylight is reserved for another day, the tomorrow that will be Egypt. The flood-lit metropolitan expanse of the modern airport should never be allowed to deceive, for once outside its immediate environs darkness dominates once more. Peering out of the coach windows allows limited visibility. The illuminated bill board, occasional Kalesh, faded hotel facades, scurrying pedestrians and the occasional donkey, are all that can be identified with any degree of certainty.

With hotel registration complete we were taken to our rooms. Directions would have been far too complicated. Sometimes on footpath, sometimes on roadway, up the steep Egyptian curbs and on through shrub-lined walkways we pursued our goal. Tired from travel and at this point separated from luggage, I wondered if the porter would ever find my room and if he did how long it would take him. Eventually, a key was put in a lock, a door opened, and bathed again in bright light, I stood in the entrance to my room. With the tip duly delivered I began the long wait for my luggage. Its arrival woke me up. With breakfast scheduled for four hours time I fell to wondering if I might have to get a taxi to take me to the dining room in the morning.

Dawn always seems to beat you to it, however early you rise and this morning was no exception. With case repacked and placed outside the door it was off to retrace the circuitous route traversed the night before. Oh, what a difference the daylight makes. I found myself in the midst of a beautiful garden with pools, flower beds, shrubs and neatly trimmed hedges. The deception of the darkness was dispelled in the glory of a morning garden. The time of departure arrived too soon but alas it was delayed whilst a search party set out to find my luggage.

Forgotten Sounds

An early morning stroll along the Luxor Corniche, before the heat begins to bite, is a pleasant way to start the day. You can watch the ferry disgorge its West Bank work force, see the dirty boat collect the rubbish from the cruisers and see the bags that missed the boat float on down the Nile. The cruisers too disgorge their clientele, who with eagerness that will have disappeared by noon, climb with gay abandon the tortuous steps to gain the coaches that will take them to their appointed sites, 'before it gets too hot!' Sellers on bicycles, bearing bread and nuts mingle among the people though no one seems to buy. A sadness comes over on occasion as you watch the hot air balloons, caught by some current sent from the desert by that malevolent god, Seth, take them to Luxor Airport rather than the Valley of the Kings. A taxi would have been much cheaper, even had you been overcharged and conceded defeat in the baksheesh war.

As the sun goes down, in that spectacular glow that seems reserved for this most amenable of places, the scene has changed completely. The traffic to the ferry now straggles like a skein of wild geese, tired from a long migration route. As some near the jetty they begin to run, others too tired, do not mind being overtaken. The cruisers now seem ready to relax and sleep. Sporadic lights appear until the curtains are closed and from time to time you glimpse the passengers whose numbers seem too sparse for such vast vessels. Balloons have given way to the horse drawn Kalesh as the chosen mode of transport through the town. The pavements seem deserted save for the forlorn felucca captain still extolling Banana Island and his cheap prices. Shoe Shine Boys bemused at all the sandals sit crossed legged and lean against the parapet. The Temple floodlights begin to dominate the scene. Fewer and fewer tourists are to be seen as this is the time for the evening dinner.

Pausing in the leisurely walk we stop and sit on the marble seats that give such splendid views across the river, also a pleasant warmth to the posterior, for they have acted as Day Storage Heaters. It is the sound that demands attention. It is not being made by any mechanical source, nor is it a man-made symphony. Nature has created it and I have heard it before somewhere. Then it dawns. It is the quintessential English evening suburban sound of fifty years ago, when we had the same extravaganza created by the humble House Sparrow. Strange to think that you have to come all the way to Egypt to recapture sounds of an English childhood. Long may their Sparrows thrive.

Pride and Prejudice

The brochure arrives and with an eager sense of anticipation, the white envelope is quickly torn open. There it is, the result of many hours of work by a dedicated team, having sought much inspiration from previous punters and their photographs. Pages are turned to look for those adventures that will provide excitement and leave memories to supply the dotage. Choices are made, friends consulted, diaries reviewed and then final decisions made.

When the booking forms are completed and the deposits paid, there remains the wait. Sometimes it is only a matter of weeks but more often it is months. Part of the joy of travel is of course, the anticipation. Making the plans, sorting the wardrobe, servicing the cameras, and arranging to get to the airport are all part of the essentials, beside pills and potions.

There is a game that some of us like to play after check-in at the airport has been accomplished. It is called 'Spot the other travellers in your party'. I really felt for this lady pushing the wheelchair around the duty free but my consolation was that they would surely not be on our trip. I began to get a little nervous when they were sitting in the departure lounge and I thought, 'surely not'. The leader did his rounds and gathered together his flock and lo and behold, there was the lady pushing the gentleman in a wheelchair. I certainly got that wrong and paid the price in the days to come. We also got another wrong. When dressed in desert-coloured clothes, somehow he didn't look the part. Looks deceive and he proved to be the life and soul, keeping morale high throughout the trip. And this brings me to the crux of this aside. Someone else was very worried.

This time we had arrived at our destination, Luxor, boarded the 4x4s next day and begun our deep desert excursion. The conversation began quite innocently as she said, "You know we have a vicar in this party? We shall have to be careful what we say. Have any of you any idea who it might be?"

At this point we were bumping along indistinguishable desert tracks and beginning to enter into the spirit of the expedition. "Well at least he isn't in this vehicle, we know that," she said with some authority. She began to go through those riding in the other vehicles first. Her lot eventually fell on an older man who she surmised fitted the bill by his looks. However, there was still a degree of uncertainty and she started to take us through her thoughts concerning the vehicle we were in. "No, you are too young and you are still a student", she said eliminating my son. "You're a lady and I know you're not a vicar", was her next assessment of her travelling companion. "This is your father and he is not a vicar", she postulated this time. "So no, he is not in this vehicle then." She continued. "I shall have to start again as I am determined to get to the bottom of this issue".

By now my son and I could contain ourselves no longer. The strain was beginning to tell on our faces and looking around she screamed, "I don't believe it, that's your Dad and he's the Vicar. I've been sitting next to him for the whole journey!"

False Teeth

We have a favourite day out in Luxor. It is the day-trip up the Nile to Dendera on the Lotus, a small cruise boat that should take up to 100 people, though I have known it to take many more. Operated then by the Iberotel Hotel, it can be booked at the desk, (which is cheaper.) It is a leisurely twelve-hour cruise up and down the Nile, bank watching, I call it. With favourite seating secured by early arrival, we settle down and await other guests bussed in from the many hotels that advertise the trip. Hot air balloons have grown in number from the first one or two some years ago to my last count of fourteen. They make for a very pleasant sight as dawn breaks across the Theban Hills. At around 7am the gangplank is noisily raised and the boat casts off. Depending on the season and the temperature, passengers either huddle under the canvas awning or rush to the sun beds on the upper deck.

"Can I sit here, alongside you?" the lady asked. I agreed, but later wished that another solution had been found. "It is my first time to Egypt and I'm travelling all alone," she continued, without pause for breath. "My friends were very surprised when I told them where I was going and they commended me for my bravery. It is wonderful to meet all these other brave people. I thought I would be very lonely. I've no idea what to do or see in Luxor and I don't really know why I came in the end, but the brochures looked so pretty and they didn't say anything about any dangers."

It began to dawn on me that this was going to be a very one-sided conversation.

She continued. "You see, I lost my hubby a few years ago and we have no children and I am not short of money and I am beginning to like travel. My friends don't like to go where I go and don't seem to want to holiday with me but I'm not going to let that worry me. I meet such nice people and now I go away three or four times a year. I would love to have a companion to travel with me and I have asked some, but no one has yet agreed."

I called to my wife. "Are you alright darling?" It seemed necessary for me to establish the fact that I was married at this point.

The lady continued. "Where are we going? Have you been there before? How hot will it get? Shall we have any food? Is that the West Bank where the terrorists are? How do they cross the river?"

She kept going. There was no time to answer any question before the next had been articulated. But now it was the direction they were taking that began to worry me.

"I will let you into a secret," she confided. I wondered what was coming. "When I was younger and my hubby was alive he persuaded me to have three of my teeth capped with gold. I don't think it would worry me too much if they kidnapped me but I've heard that they will go for my gold fillings and I could not tolerate that!"

The National Bank

You have to pass the Bank if you are walking at the lower end of the Corniche to where it bears left and becomes the start of the highway to Luxor Bridge. It is no mystery to natives of Luxor what hours the Bank opens its doors but to those of us who visit infrequently, a degree of confusion abounds. Then again it was Ramadan and that added yet another dimension.

Passing by on the way to the Iberotel Hotel, there were approximately thirty men crowded round the doors of the Bank at the top of six steps. I supposed that in a moment it would be open for business and took no notice. Checking a few details at hotel reception we moved through to the gardens to view the swimming pool and watch the sunset across the Nile. It was a scene of calm and quiet. The view looked ready for some photos, and that took up more time than anticipated. Later than we planned we turned to make our way back along the Corniche to our hotel. By now it was almost dark and we chose to walk on the side of the road away from the river, hopefully avoiding too much hassle from the hustlers selling their wares, including boat rides. Crossing the road at the roundabout is always fun as you can place no confidence in the traffic obeying either lights or directions. As we rounded the corner we could see that the crowd outside the Bank had grown considerably in the time that had elapsed, now numbering more like a hundred. Just when would it open? To get around the seething mass we had to use the middle of the road and compete with the horse-drawn carriages, called Kaleshes,

107

also cars and coaches. I stood amazed at what was going on and looked alarmed at the security guard on duty. He raised his hands in a gesture of despair and then bust out laughing. Faces were flattened against glass and bars that comprised the main doors of the Bank. Pressure from behind forced the men forward. Had this been at a football stadium all the alarm bells would have been sounding. But this is Egypt and men wanting money.

I could only watch. Suddenly the glass and bars gave way and the human tide surged forward. Those at the front fell as the surge at the back gained new momentum. For sure the doors had been opened but pity the man brave enough to have been at the front of the queue. Now those at the front were lying on the steps in the entrance as those behind used them at stepping stones to gain admittance. Wondering what lessons could be learned I realised there were none, for this fracas would be repeated over and over, every day of the fast as it had been for years and the security guard would stand and watch and laugh. Perhaps there is a moral here that if you want your money, never be at the front of the scrum.

Plastic Holiday

Somehow he had the look of a young plastic surgeon about him - trim figure, manicured nails, pedicured feet and sculpted hair. Surely the ladies with him must be here for tummy tucks. She would be mother, acceding more to the passing years but these could never be mistaken for her daughters. Hard they tried to condense the flesh into the cotton confinement of the bikini but alas without much success. Yet here was nothing that some careful rearrangement or realignment could not improve.

They laughed, joked and splashed about together in the pool with a seeming expectation that a day would soon be when a longing for a fresh figure would be realised. You could sense the trust they had in the debonair young man. Their eyes gave the game away. To him they deferred both in the water and out of it. When he was gone, for what and where was not disclosed, they seemed a little nervous. When he returned confidence seemed to rise and muted nerves gave way to laughter once again.

I did wonder, at what cost and at what profit was this deal done and would the insurance clause for 'dangerous sport' really surrender value if it all should come apart?

The skills of surgeons have greatly improved with the passage of time. Whereas once his art was clearly visible through patterned scars, today he works along the ridges and the valleys of the surface skin, leaving little evidence that he has ever passed that way. It takes a practiced eye and a good light to follow his handiwork these days. So, when some scars stand out so visibly, questions are of course, asked. What was the level of his skill? How long ago was he at work? Was he hard-pressed for time? Did his mood or demeanour have anything to do with it? There are other questions too. Just what does that scar represent and is something no longer there that once was visible?

The norm would be that the scar would disclose an invisible removal, maybe something taken from the inside or indeed something introduced from the outside. But on occasion it is known that plastic surgery goes wrong and what is left belies the craftsman's skill. I have often reflected what would be disclosed around a pool if scars were counted and operations disclosed. Would such a survey be of any scientific or academic use? I have my doubts there is a hidden PhD here, but one thing is for sure, stay close and you will overhear the post-operative history of many maturing citizens. Poolside talk is so disclosing.

"They managed to get all of it out."

"Just how old is that hip?"

"Three knees you say? What happened to the one that got away?"

At first glance something seemed to have gone decidedly wrong. For a moment it was hard to place. Then it dawned - her breasts were in the wrong place. That is to say they were far too low. What had begun as uplift resulted in downfall.

However, she displayed no embarrassment at all. Indeed, her posture spoke only of pride, for what the observers of the fallen figure did not realise was that this was not the first nor would it be the last exciting excursion she would enjoy. The fruits of compensation would last her for many a year to come and take her to yet further and further exotic locations.

Young Companions

Clearly they were on a voyage of discovery. Every look, every movement, every touch, every glance and smile said loudly, exploration! Still in the flush of youth, it was the first time for both to be away from home and both to be together. Family and peer groups were left far behind. Now they were on their own and they could begin to discover so much more about each other. Every day saw a little more tenderness and a little less embarrassment. He moved the lounger to the shade whilst she smiled. He led the way into the pool as if to test the temperature. He ordered from the bar and made sure he paid the bill. You could sense the growing ease in the relationship, less stress more understanding. Less talk giving way to gentle caress.

Now today she is all alone at the poolside. She moves her own lounger, tests the water temperature herself and even orders and pays for her own cool drink. Has he just overslept and is she just left to wait? Her purposefulness seems to tell another story. Some unfortunate event has overtaken the budding love. All is later revealed as he is seen to return later in the day holding another young companion by the hand.

The 'Opening of the Mouth' and Other Rituals

As all scholars of mummification know, for that process of preservation ultimately to succeed, there has to be performed a ceremony entitled, 'The Opening of the Mouth'. For a Pharaoh, only one could do that. The successor. Using prescribed instruments but possessing no acquired experiential skill, the task was to set free the embalmed to partake, in the afterlife, of all the goodies surrounding him, both in mummified reality and as exquisitely portrayed in tomb decoration.

A contemporary ritual can be observed in the same proximity at Thebes, which is essential for entering the arena of contemporary life. This ritual involves not the careful wrapping but rather the careful unwrapping, to which the title 'The Unveiling of the Flesh' might be given.

No self-respecting widow of advancing years would be seen to have arrived without having completed the ritual of 'The Unveiling of the Flesh' beside the hotel pool. Age has bestowed no favours nor made the slightest concession. But, to have arrived in the nether world of ageing vanity, it is deemed essential for the jaded whiteness to be exposed to the browning of the sun.

Each morning he is there, preened and waiting for something which at the poolside, could only lead to one conclusion, the sun. The ritual of sunbathing is about to begin.

He is replete with small backpack, whose contents he is quick to divulge. Laid out neatly beside the second of the two prepared sun-beds are the lotions and the potions, needing several orange-coloured containers of various sizes to do them justice; the small cloth, neatly folded for some undisclosed purpose, the reading book, a novel appearing to be chosen for its size rather than its content. Then there is the small silver tube containing the designer sun-reflectors. The purse or rather pouch for it had begun by hanging round the neck. There is a container of cash to buy the many drinks and finally the draw-string bag, whose contents remains a secret as no eye, except that of the owner, knows what is inside. It seems that now the wait can begin in earnest. Can the 'He' be waiting for his 'She'?

Not more than two sun-beds away each morning she is there, kitted out for the sunbathing and swimming ritual. She too lays out an almost identical display of the day's requirements, as comprehensive in its nature as his. She too, begins a wait. This time is the 'She' waiting for the 'He'?

As succeeding days disclose, the waiting time varies, but it always errs on the side of long. The waiting time includes the briefest of conversations across the empty beds.

Brief though these exchange are, they are often repeated. As time passes on, the pool is graced with a rather beautiful display that could have caught the judge's eye in any synchronised swimming event.

Now, the divided beds abandoned, together side by side, the wanting has been taken out of the waiting. A new relationship is born.

Sound Re-Enforcement

Standing in the pool with just the head exposed to the searing sun, sounds seem magnified or, as the purists would say, reinforced. Poolside conversation is easily overheard even by those who would claim some level of hearing impairment.

Suddenly, it was as though the poolside itself was shaking, as his great weight accelerated towards the water. The first view was of his underside as he passed overhead. The shorts had little to command attention but ah, the skin colour, that was something different. Instead of the Anglo-Saxon shade of pink, there was a bluish hue.

Then came the crash. In no way could it be described as splash! A deep hole was hammered into the water's surface as he disappeared. A consequent tsunami raced across the water, only to hit the poolside wall and rush, returning again to fill the crater his body had carved out. The face might well be protected from the sun but now nothing offered protection from the water. When sight returned he was just beginning to surface. That bluish body hue now left only his face exposed and that was covered with long unkempt hair of equal length both on head and chin. The picture gradually became clearer. As he descended for a second time, from neck to ankles, he was closely tattooed leaving no space for the artist to exercise his craft on this canvas again. As he arose and descended yet again, the returning tsunami decreased in magnitude and it became apparent that all those swimming seemed to have been washed to the water's edge. Then he rose erect at the mid-depth of the pool and the wonder of his picture gallery could be seen in all its glory. The bikers' patterns were all there as was the 'Hells' Angels' motif.

With a deep sense of apprehension all eyes were fixed on him, anticipating the moment when he would disappear beneath the water, for all were gripped with the same fear, would his Harley and his friends be following?

The Headmaster and his Wife

Beside her 'honourable plumpness' (my memory fails me, I cannot recall the source of this descriptive phrase) he was quite diminutive. She seemed as tall as he was short yet both looked well wined and dined.

School was out and now they could be seen together. Comparative size was an embarrassment they just could not face before the phalanx of pupils. Here discretion was abandoned.

For every two steps he took she could comfortably manage one and this created the impression that he was running to keep up. To see her face his was almost vertical. But it was the rimless spectacles precariously arranged on his well-sculpted nose that disclosed his occupation. Years of looking up to pupils, many years his junior and looking down at the examination papers, so frequently marked with red exclamations, all helped generate the sense of alertness that pervaded his whole persona. It was as though, at a moments notice the spring would uncoil and a devastating authority would be unleashed, which would cause the assembled pupils to realise that an unknown fate was about to fall upon them.

But here beside the pool it was oh so different. He now came under the authority of a higher mortal. Her imposing presence dominated all. If she had worn the trilby instead of him, she it would have been who would have raised it to the passing ladies. An expression of a faded gentrification that retained its last vestige in his small form.

Holding hands they walked with an air of superiority

among the loungers laden with their recumbent areas of exposed flesh. You could almost hear her say, "George, keep your eyes on me." Indeed, there was enough there to claim his attention for some considerable time.

The Bikini

Seemingly less popular around the pool these days, the bikini still has its exponents. Maybe it is the 'Saga Syndrome', as youth gives way to age but I fear not. Those advocates of the bikini's allure have, somewhere along the line lost, if they ever had, the purpose of the adornment. Was it there to conceal or to expose?

Around the pool a high degree of uncertainty was evidenced. The proponents of the concealing theory valiantly made something so small attain almost impossible feats, whilst those of the exposure theory allowed visibility to be given to areas that had not seen the light of day for some considerable time.

And evidence of pre-holiday shopping was apparent, where deliberate choice or reckless abandon determined size and shape. Clearly the mirror had only fleetingly been consulted and its advice either overlooked or totally ignored.

So too was the rest of the holiday wardrobe, apparently. The redness of the previous days exposure told a tale that revealed a yet smaller size had been purchased but courage had failed in the first instance when deciding what to wear.

Buddha-like she sat recumbent on the lounger, as roll upon roll of flesh descended, settled and began to soak up the sun. The shades added just the right touch of modernity.

Husband is small by comparison and clearly knows his place. He who foots the bill gets to choose so very little.

In normal life she would not be seen dead like this. But here, far from home and quite unknown to all, she can become the person she would most like to be, were it not for the facts of flesh.

In another life she could be a Matron or anything below that status, once so highly prized. Authority exudes from her bearing, as patients quake before her and dare not tell a lie.

Meanwhile husband sits beside her, beside the pool and is haunted by one thought. Just how did she manage to persuade him to buy the black bikini?

The Repellent

Flies can be such a nuisance. Time spent disturbing them is so tiresome, as they want to explore such inaccessible places. However, one thing has always puzzled me. When a fly is seen upon a towel, a book or table, why the urge to frighten it away? When occupied there at least it cannot be annoying you.

Some, however, select a choice of repellents to keep these tiny monsters at bay. They spray the body and any surrounding static objects in the vain hope that the creeping sensation across the flesh will be an experience of the past.

Just what is it that is proposed to be repelled? Carefully she related where she had bought it and how its virtues had been expounded. One thing however was not attempted. Unlike the perfume counters awash with a mixture of fragrances ready to be tested on a variety of pressure points, there was a distinct absence of testers at the pesticide stand.

Testing on pressure points was neither banned nor recommended. It was just something no one ever did with insecticide, that is until thousands of miles from home they encountered the offending insects. Then, out came the spray, everything in range was covered with foul smelling invisible droplets and all flies disappeared. That was not all. What she failed to realise was that all too soon, she too was totally alone.

Flies are not so bashful about visiting the conveniences. Near the pool, discreetly signed, the conveniences are situated behind a screen of bougainvillea and lattice woodwork. Ah, how convenient. To discover the great relief and pleasure that they provide, I suggest you sit beside the pool alongside the walkway to these discreet palaces, as I was forced so to do one day. You may study several things from this perspective as I discovered, finding that the only spot remaining by the pool was adjacent to this rat run. I say 'rat run' in that it is so descriptive of the route commuters choose to avoid the congestion and frustration of the rush hour traffic. There are so many similarities here.

First, there are those who seem to be both in a hurry and yet are moving so carefully. Second, there are those whose speed dictates the need for all to clear a path, for determination is written all over their faces.

Third, I noticed those who felt a need to be so discreet about their movements that they felt that no one should know of the destination of their circuitous journeying. They would come by a meandering route, which for all its twists and turns, led ultimately to the same place.

But perhaps most distinctive of all was the look upon their faces. Contortions can disfigure the most distinguished of countenances and the variety displayed gave all uniqueness.

Not so upon the return leg of the journey. All uniqueness and individuality of countenance has given way to commonality. All contortions have departed. Strained and furrowed brows are now relaxed. All has given way to signs of satisfaction and contentment. The smiles of pleasure and confidence all borne out the fact of a job well done.

Life and Death

To whom are the signs of advanced pregnancy an embarrassment? Carrying the rounded contours of the sublime fact seems to be a badge of honour. For most it is carried with considerable pride.

The poolside displays come in a rich variety of shapes and sizes from the petite one who seems outrageously large, to the largess of the form that seems to be carried without a care.

Contained as they are in a variety of costumes, nothing can disguise the wondrous event that new life is confined within an older life and release will come at birth. The poolside does not lie. Those most embarrassed by the apparent advanced stages of pregnancy are, of course the men, whose largeness and rotundity often outstrips that of the ladies.

I heard at the poolside.

"Yes, that's right, we're on a mission."

"Oh, what is that?'"

"I have my late husband here, only his ashes you understand, to scatter at Hatshepsut's Temple on the West Bank. You know, the undertaker charged me £800 for a very special container in which to bring them over here. It is supposed not to show on the X-ray. He said on no account to ask for permission about anything in Egypt and certainly not to dispose of my husband. I was so worried at the airport that I might have to open my case. I couldn't tell them I had my husband in there. And what if they found him? What might they charge me with? He has already cost me an extra £800. There's more. We now have to pay for a taxi to get him over there to the West Bank!"

Lonely?

If it moved she videoed it, or so I thought, then realised it didn't have to move to catch her eye. She videoed everything before her. She entered the hotel and passing through the metal detector, camera still whirring quietly away, she advanced on reception and began to pan. It was then that her eyes lighted upon the map. Some three metres tall, it showed the outline of Egypt bisected by the Nile. The only reference points beside the international boundaries and the river were a series of yellow lights. At least they were yellow when switched on. They were there simply to indicate where other hotels of the same chain were situated. Now with calm deliberation she slowly scanned up and down the vertical map of the river. Safe in the knowledge that she had captured something for somebody, she seemed satisfied.

But just how would she describe what this was supposed to be when, within a mere hundred metres she could have videoed the real thing? Such was the dilemma faced on the day trip from Hurghada to the Valley of the Kings with only a brief pause for lunch in a Luxor before the whirlwind trip continued to Karnak and Luxor temples.

She had got up at an ungodly hour, boarded one of the fifty or so coaches that would take Red Sea visitors to a few of the Nile sites in a seemingly endless convoy, just to be able to say Luxor had been 'done'. Visions of the convoy pausing briefly for refreshments at the only 'rest house' on route and the queue for the facilities flooded the mind. It is a six hour journey either way.

Hastily snatched pictures would be the prize gleaned with great discomfort.

I have to call him 'Lonely', for that is what my ears see as my eyes speak to me. Yes, that is the right way round, for all my senses fused in unison.

Every morning he was there. No matter what time we arrived beside the pool, there he was. Purely out of interest I once tried to get there before him but I failed. Could it be that there was some residual Germanic blood coursing his arteries and veins, that could be the explanation? By years he looked in early thirties but that did not seem to provide a clue to his being consistently alone for long periods of time. Bereavement crossed my mind. Maybe an attempt to vacate the present moment of pain to wrestle inwardly with grief. His countenance was not consistent with that explanation.

Yet there is another type of bereavement, which comes about as one partner chooses another, leaving aloneness as a legacy. There was no ring on either hand or fainter shade disclosing where one might have been. Yet trying to read that sort of thing today rarely makes any sense.

What was haunting him to the extent that he would spend these long hours unoccupied? Here the mind could race away with imaginary tales filled with disastrous dangers making him a sole survivor.

But truth began to dawn after about a week of watching by the pool. It was triggered by the deliberate attention to detail, which he took when performing the ritual application of the factor '5'. As day succeeded day the trunks were readjusted and it looked as though even comfort was not a consideration as constant attempts were made to expose the more unexposable. And there it was at last, an almost perfect tan. Both density and colour were consistent, a richly bronzed Adonis for many to admire.

Yet there remained one further, haunting, unanswered question. Who, each day, anointed his unreachable?

To Know and to be Known

All have seen you before, even if it is your first visit. Room service, waiters, pool-side attendants, all have known you even when it's your first time on the scene. They seem to suffer from what I call Memory Reversal Syndrome, a quite different type of MRS. They remember things yet to be and all faces of the future. "I remember you!" is but a beginning.

It is of course a gimmick to ingratiate themselves and you have the option of playing the game yourself or, to put it plainly, 'get in first'. In my case it goes like this.

"Don't I know you?"

"Oh yes, I remember you from my last trip, you were the incompetent waiter who could never get things right. You told me all about your twelve children and sick wife, trying hard to gain my sympathy and an even larger tip".

Not understanding that flow of English he is delighted with the supposed complement.

What of course he doesn't know is that when it comes to tipping, I have devised a system. I make an early decision as to what I shall donate. As time progresses and the service unfolds I bring into play my system of deductions. It becomes a pattern of diminishing returns.

"Alas," I say to him, "you were the one that ended up with my last 50 piaster note."

Dressing Up

I never did discover how they 'found' Jo, an ex Tui holiday rep in Luxor, and now contracted to my travel company. At the airport she was awaiting her punters when I first saw her.

The second time was at the poolside. Now she was a BBC extra in the Carter/Tut extravaganza being there filmed. Disappearing into a 'Tardis' like construction, which once provided space for hotel guest 'activities', in a simple but practical dress, she emerged five minutes later in a plain gown reaching to her feet. In the intervening moments she had gained at least a stone in weight. Now starring as Lord Carnarvon's nurse, she looked so right for the part, with the elegance and grace of a former age, save for the costume number inelegantly pinned to her right sleeve. '45A Jo' it read. Now she turned to have the belt fitted and, alas, all was revealed. The gown was for a different figure, needing at least another half metre of material to complete her circumnavigation. There exposed below the bra and above the underskirt was a wide expanse of flesh. The word here for the nurse must surely be, "Never show My Lord your back. He just might expire prematurely."

"How times have changed", they say.

"Luxor, this year ladies."

"Where is that?"

"We fly from Manchester."

"But that will be expensive!"

"Not as much as Blackpool dear, since they put up the

prices."

So it was that they descended to the poolside, Luxor, Egypt. From where did they get those costumes. Got to be somewhere way 'oop' North. I know South Africa is called the rainbow nation but this is far from that homeland and this is material not people. I also know that new electronic apparatus boasts production of hundreds of new colours but even those are not a patch on this. Even flowers and candy were not arranged like such as these. Of course it was the voices and the accents that gave them away to their fellows from the British Isles. Proud of their regional accents they minded not the heads that turned their way. And, enjoy it, "we are going to," they told each other as though somehow it was compulsory. Even the temperature of the water was not going to be allowed to spoil the fun. With shrieks and shouts they be-sported themselves in the open air pool.

This was their day, their week, and you can forget about 'Tut's Tomb', 'The West Bank', 'Temples and Tombs'. "It's even cheaper than Morecambe!"

We all try it at some stage. Some are more successful than others and there is no more opportune time to think about it than before a holiday. Well before preferably, as she was to find out. It all started at the 'trying on' stage when last year's wardrobe came under scrutiny. Much to her dismay there was only one long skirt that would comfortably fasten in the right place. It would have to be a crash diet, a visit to the charity shops and a limited expenditure in the retail store to solve this year's problems. The issue was however, time. As always she had started late and more in hope than expectation too. There were only four weeks to go before the adventure would begin. How much weight can one shed in that time, she wondered. Having heard about those who had managed one or two pounds per week, she allowed an unwarranted optimism to overtake her. Things began well, as they always do in the beginning, but it was not long before the starvation tactics ceased their magic. Time was running out. Back to last year's wardrobe once more! Alas the problem had not improved. It was in the hotel dining room in Luxor that I overheard the question. "Why is it dear, that when you try to slim, you always seem to lose weight in all the wrong places?"

Ankhesenamun

Had she lived she would be very old by now, Tutankhamun's child bride, beautiful to behold in multi-coloured radiance, depicted in numerous marvellous inlays of precious stones displayed in museum isolation.

But her replica, sitting here beside the pool is old and I'm no ageist. One wonders why, in retrospect, so much trouble is taken. She follows the Egyptian style and patterns. Tall and skinny, sorry I mean slim, she begins the process of disrobing. First the skirt, once diaphanous but now somewhat faded, to reveal, well, I'm not sure what, for it really takes some finding.

Pretensions to purple but now more grey, the bottom half hides little. The jacket but can it really be called that, is truly amazing. Grandma's crochet, which was more holes than substance, comes to mind. Here the large holes are holding multicoloured plastic discs representing those semi precious materials, gathered from great distance at considerable cost, to adorn Pharaoh's palaces and person. It outshines anything else at the poolside and hangs flaccid, halfway down this seated form, to well below the knees. This predates the Jacob's Coat that today does not get a mention in Egyptological circles, for it seems that even the Jews are themselves expunging from their nation's history, a sojourn in Egypt as the Exodus becomes another myth. This jacket, which I got quite lost describing, rattles as it is released. What it reveals again seems to be hiding very little. But when fully revealed it also had aspirations to purple.

The sudden splash took everyone by surprise. She had dived into the water and all that is now visible is the bun. High on the head, it could be real but I have my doubts.

As she emerges from the pool I think I have seen her somewhere before. I wrack my brain as short term memory loss again takes its toll but in a moment when I am not thinking about it I remember. It was the mummy room in the great Cairo Museum. The wrinkling of the skin gave away the game.

Darker Shade of Pale

It was their first trip to Egypt. Ever since they had known each other, about a year, it was their dream. He had come from Africa but it was via a circuitous route. West Africans know little about Egypt and Egyptians are not too comfortable to be called Africans. It could be said that the learning curve would be steep. For him that was true but for her a different reality played out. She was from the English Shires, as far removed from Africans and Arabs as you can get. Her education had included some Egyptology but only at a very elementary level. As so often is the case, a quickening takes place in childhood and youth, which if nourished later by some further Egyptian incident, can grow and blossom into a consuming passion. So it was with her and as she came under his spell, it was not long before he too felt the same quickening. For education he had come and it was proving its worth. However, his family back home in Ghana, who had made sacrifices to send him to the UK, was not so happy when he disclosed his intentions not to return to provide but rather to be adopted by his English hosts and settle among them through education, employment, and eventual marriage.

So here they were, seated beside each other on the plane, full of anticipations. For a Ghanaian, he was not as dark as some and for the English maiden, she had lost her paleness. Since falling for him in a serious way, she had spent many hours under the lamps in the tanning studios. Darker and darker she became until it was apparent what she was after. The fact however remained, for no matter how long she spent under the lamps she would never match the richness and the depth of his shade.

Demise of the White Coat

The one constant of the National Health Service is change. So it was, that just before we left for an Egyptian Holiday, we learned the latest one. It is a tradition, it is an institution, it is a badge of honour, it is the physician's White Coat. Worn with pride upon the passing of the appropriate examinations, written, practical, theoretical, and viva voce, the student has it washed and pressed to take forward into the world of proper jobs. As patients, we look out for it to distinguish the one with all the knowledge, the mystique, and maybe the cure. He is to be addressed as 'Doctor,' that is until he becomes elevated to Consultant, and then for some reason, known only to the medical profession, he becomes 'Mr' again.

Now this White Coat is to be abolished and what a problem it creates. What is to happen to all those white coats? Seldom do they wear out and they do not fade with the passing of time. There is an awful permanence about them, an indestructible quality.

He had planned the trip for some time and certainly long before he knew of the decree that told of the abandonment of the white coat. His wife was so enthusiastic. She it was who finally made the booking for Egypt and obtained the books from the local library that were the required reading before the event. They spent time talking about it, planning it, researching it, and watching the relevant Discovery and National Geographical Channels to whet their appetites. Packing was left to her, as well it might for she it was who had the time. Allowances were made for the heat but a minimal amount of money was spent on a new wardrobe. Arrival came at last and here they were, in Egypt. The clothes travelled in now abandoned, they stepped out in their latest holiday collection that would grace any fashion catwalk. Carefully yet secretly, she had modified those garments designed to enclose medical inscrutability and converted them into a matching pair of beautifully tailored jackets designed to repel the heat of Egypt. At least two would be saved for posterity.

Mummy is Paying

Clearly they were very much in love. Here there was no equality of the sexes. He waited on her as though his life depended on it and who knows, it might have done. He showed her to her seat he eased her chair so that she could sit comfortably he called the waiter and ordered tea for her, then coffee for himself together they walked the breakfast buffet bar and he waited for her to take first choice returning to their places once more he offered her the chair, waiting until she was comfortable, then he took up his place. Discussion concerning the day's itinerary would be the conversation over the meal and everything looked perfect. However, all was not as it seemed.

There was a table for two near the one they occupied but they had ignored that, preferring a table to accommodate four. Continually they were looking around, as though anticipating something that had not yet happened. Unhurried too it seemed, as though they were awaiting something else to transpire. At the entrance to the dining hall, the ever vigilant staff member, whose duty it was to account for all the guests and their room numbers attending the meal, spies another latecomer. Taking details on a slip of paper before making the entry in the official register, full of smiles, she takes the slightly overdressed lady to the table where the young couple are seated, eases the chair and invites her to sit down.

It is now that a noticeable change comes over the faces of the young ones. All the smiles have disappeared, the eye contact has gone, and there is a distinct stiffness about their attitude to each other. Mother has arrived. It is her mother, for they are sharing a room. The days itinerary will clearly be for three now. The truth becomes apparent. Since Mummy is paying for this trip then she has every right to come herself.

Flash the Waiter

I call him 'Flash' as a term of affection. My first encounter with him was just that. He was there one minute and the next he was gone. But just as the lightening leaves the roar of thunder echoing across the heavens, so the rapidity of his movement left shock waves reverberating in my mind. How did he do that?

Normally they are a phlegmatic bunch, the waiters that populate the hotels of Luxor, mainly emanating from the West Bank, across the Nile. That is why he stood out, or at least one of the reasons why he did. Another reason was that he stood head and shoulders above all the others. It was clear that he was above average in every respect, for his provided wardrobe was a good size and a half too small. This gave the impression that he was still growing and would soon need to be resized. It also meant that his biceps appeared to have a degree of menace about them, that left a taste of fear lingering in the throat after conversation. You would always want him to be your friend and choosing sides you would always pick him first.

When it came to his ability to perform his tasks it quickly became apparent why he was hired before all the other contenders. It was his speed, agility and dexterity. Only one word could be used to describe his movement through the dining room and that word is 'flow.' From kitchen to the tables his movement was unimpeded as was the return journey. No matter what he was called upon to accomplish during the course of that itinerary, it was all achieved through one fluid motion. And then there was the speed.

Others, ministering to the variety of guests needs were overtaken again and again. What created this sensation of rapidity began with his eyes. Large as they were, it meant that when they were rolled, large areas of white were exposed. The movement of his torso followed the movement of his eyes and all this was before he had engaged his legs. It was a leaning forward against the perpendicular that gave the impression of movement before he had even started on his duty run. Finally the legs were connected to the process and the flow became apparent in the forward motion. Almost touching his right ear, arm aloft, he held the tray, sometimes empty, but more often laden with the remnants of the diners' meal, piled high with crockery. His stature summarised his strength.

Bending low, as if to whisper in my ear, he introduced me to forgotten phrases of his native tongue. "Sabah il-kheer," was followed by my feeble, "sabah in-nur" and I knew that I had found a friend and moreover a protector.

Company Promotion

Which came first, the marble slab in sun or the night storage heater with electricity? Cool to the posterior, as you sit and gaze across the Nile in the early dawn light and very warm to that same portion of your anatomy as you watch the sun disappear at nightfall, those shaded slabs, conveniently situated along the Luxor Corniche, serving as both seats and viewing points, are where I love to watch the world go by.

From all across the world they come, with the 'lingua franca' broken English. You try to answer their many questions, but oh, if only you could understand what they might be asking. Even though the travel industry has rationalised of late, there are many smaller operators that specialise in Egypt. I guess the more specialist the more expensive but you are left wondering how much, apart from the numerous tips, really gets to the folk who appear to need it most. Likewise the hotels change hands and become part of fewer and fewer chains that then try with great difficulty, to shed their names and adopt new ones. It's the labels on the 'carry on' bags, that double up as 'rucksacks', that so often indicate the airline, tour operator or hotel chain. It's all to do with company 'logo' and promotion, I suppose. Corporate identity seems to feature too. Then sometimes there are the 'freebies'. It was this latter category that caught my eye most recently and only someone who had never been to Egypt could have come up with this one.

The Oasis of Dakhla should not be missed if you are

serious about this fascinating country and whilst there you must not miss Al-Qasr, a medieval settlement built upon Roman foundations. An ancient Islamic town, it is now abandoned and yet maintained in wonderful condition. Its proliferation of passageways, narrow and not always open to the sky, invites you to get lost.

Once alone, let your imagination do the rest and as you peer into long forsaken dwellings, inhabitants from the past will haunt you if you let them. Do find the renovated Madrassa dating from the 10th century and also the ancient Mosque. The donkey-powered grain mill should also detain you.

There is so much here and at every turn a new delight awaits the traveller, increasingly intoxicated by the seemingly never-ending succession of revelations. But, beware of the dust and of course the flies. As you emerge from the claustrophobic containment of this ancient commune, the children greet you with a delightful array of wares they try to sell. A 'must purchase', is a fly-whisk made from the fronds of the date palms. These are gathered in a woven woollen patterned grip at one end and the mass of waving wands at the other will quickly move away any fly that comes within a few feet of you.

The freebie carried by every member of a certain party to the poolside was the plastic fly swat, embellished with the company logo that came from their homeland in the West. Alas it was designed to deal with only one fly at a time and so totally inadequate for Egypt. We swear by the 'Dakhla Destroyers' as we call them, made and sold only at the Oasis.

Employment Prospects

I met him as he was settling into his new job. He was going about it in a masterful way. The eleven or so people under him all seemed a little nervous. I suppose they had every right to be so, for he had not been brought up through the ranks but as the saying goes, had been 'brought in from the outside'. There were those who resented him for this, feeling they had been overlooked both on the basis of skill and years of loyal service. There were those who resented him because of the thinking and changed procedures he brought. There were those who just resented him.

It had long been his ambition to be a senior waiter in an exclusive establishment, ever since his cousin had talked to him about what was involved, for he was one who had risen through the ranks and knew all there was to know about the trade. Thirty-two years service under his belt and still he had aspirations to make the top.

So much to do with employment opportunity depends upon what your father did before you in this country and the encouragement he gave you to follow in his footsteps. Things though are changing now. Sons dream of bigger and better things, spurred on by the television that invades the whole of Egypt from the Bedouin Tent to the New Valley homes. However, the pull to go and labour in the New Valley projects does not have about it the glamour of the Red Sea coast, the new technologies and the wider pull of affluent civilisation. Witness the Arab Spring.

His cousin went into the hotel trade in his early teens, so it was natural for him to be found an opening in the family business when the opportunity came. A job for life is still very much the way it is, if you follow in your father's footsteps. But for our ambitious employee things were to turn out differently. Sure, he began by following in his father's footsteps and all too soon was ready to assume the role laid out for him but alas here there was only room for one. He learnt the trade from the time that he could walk and how glad his father was, for he could share the more routine of duty. However, the day was coming when Father knew he would have to hand over the reins to his son, and that is literally what he did. He gave him the job of driver but not the owner of the Kalesh. His boy could now be seen cracking the whip as he stirred the mare into a gallop on the way to Karnak Temple.

Lucky for him, his day came. The vacant hotel Job was his at last.

"Is he always like this?" I asked a lowlier waiter.

"Yes Sir, he used to be a Kalesh driver and now he is driving us!"

Internationals

When hotel management decided upon evenings of international cuisine, whose benefit did they have in mind? Clearly it would be of benefit to the several chefs who would gain much new experience and add variety to what might otherwise be mundane routine. For those of us who sample the results of the culinary skills they employ, variety plays a large and important part. We certainly benefit from their flair and dexterity. But did anyone give thought to the wider implications? These are seen from time to time when the themed evenings are taken to further lengths than merely the kitchen and restaurant productions.

Polystyrene has many uses. The resulting skills in carving it can be seen in such displays as the Eiffel Tower, the Leaning Tower of Pisa, the Statue of Liberty, parts of the Acropolis and Tower Bridge. Your own geographical cognisance tells you what the theme of the night is and therefore what you might expect upon the table. On the international nights, every piece was brought into play.

It was when I saw the waiters that I realised something fresh was being brought to the eating experience. Not only were the table runners displaying the country colours of that particular night but also the waiters themselves were likewise adorned with the same colour combinations in their uniform. Were these the international football strip of the said countries involved? It gave that impression and what was designed for taste and décor now had a very racy look about it.

That would have been fine had not one of the waiters

reported for duty the next day with a large plaster under his chin. On enquiring what had happened to him I learned of a sorry tale how he ended up at the local hospital, having had a repair job done with three stitches. Had he fallen off his bike I wondered? Nothing as prosaic as that. This was a badge of honour won on the soccer field and worn with pride. For whom then did he play? A local Luxor team? An Upper Egypt eleven? Or maybe it was a representative match where he hoped to be spotted and escape the meagre hotel pay? Alas, his injury was sustained during a match of the Theban Hotel League, getting full use of the strips worn previously on the international night.

The Chaperone

"Can I take your booking please?" was the greeting of the head waiter as we entered the dining room. This proved to be an invitation to the famed Egyptian Evening on the following Saturday. The consensus was that this was simply a way of making sure that at least someone turned up. It was not the food that worried me so much as the thought of the entertainment. As one who is totally embarrassed by the Belly Dancer's approaches as she leaves the stage to 'mingle', it can be greatly compounded by the fact that the whole proceedings are videoed.

The bread was so tasty that it distracted from the nondescript 'main' dishes and the delicious 'sweets' were clearly not designed for the diabetic. As the meal progressed and those attending the 'alfresco' event increased, the music began. It was when the 'dancers' appeared that things started to go downhill. Looking old enough to know better, three men disported themselves around the stage with no seeming rhythm or pattern but vigorously waving sticks. Briefly they moved behind a screen and returned in different costumes to perform the same ritual as before. Yet again they returned from behind the screen and this time presented as a camel and his driver, who was still waving his stick. Again they did the previous two routines, or that is how it seemed to me.

Clearly this was designed for the children present and as this disfigured humped creature began his perambulations, they were delighted to participate by climbing on his back. However, the inevitable happened when the driver spotted an attractive young lady. Was there an Arabic fable equivalent to the Greek myth of 'Leda and the Swan,' which involved a damsel and a camel? Hailing most likely from South Korea, the young lady in question entered fully into the spirit of the 'entertainment' and drew the biggest round of applause heard all evening as she rode the camel's back. The dancers now deserted the stage and the tempo of the music increased which led to the one conclusion I had feared.

As a precaution, the seats furthest from the stage and in half-light, attracted our attention and that was where we sat in seeming obscurity, until we saw something begin to move in the shadows. She was dressed from head to foot in black. Being kind to the face, it was wizened. The cooks, the waiters and the members of the band, fawned over her. They found a seat, a table and a chair and then surprise, surprise, a chore! From somewhere, black plastic bags and bread were produced and her role was to fill the bags with bread and put them to one side.

On the stage, emerging from behind the band an overweight, ill clad and tired-looking lady began to try to shake something. How sad it was to my untrained eye. But for those aficionados of the art of Belly Dancing she was rated. For fifteen minutes she gyrated, shaking everything in sight and I guess some not. But we all knew what was coming when she began to descend the steps. Feeling vulnerable and under attack, I tried to make myself invisible. Alas, she advanced and as she hid behind a veil I created my own with a generous napkin, albeit white to her black and opaque for her to see through. Advancing still, she drew nearer and nearer. The video lights illuminating the scene, the cameraman gaining his position of advantage, she was poised to throw herself upon me when from the huddled mass of black, still filling bags with bread, came a distinct clearing of the throat. Thank God for chaperones and in particular this one who had clearly taken a dislike to me. The Belly Dancer retreated and I lowered my napkin veil, calm was restored and I gently smiled back at the black mound.

The Mobile

It was hot. By that I mean the temperature raced up to 100 degrees on the old Fahrenheit scale and stayed there for most of the day. For someone from a Northern European country that is hot.

There was only one recourse and that was the pool. Of course, it was the preferred option of the majority, so space around it was at a premium. So too were towels, indeed I did see a L50 Egyptian note changing hands for an extra towel. How the attendants must love these hot days! All was now quiet save for the sound of the birds, with the House Crow's coarse call tending to dominate the more delicate song of the dove and Sun Bird. Books were to hand, displaying the rich variety of languages present. Eyes were tending to close and the ice buckets, cooling water, were everywhere. All was a scene of peace and tranquillity.

Yet like so many good things it did not last long. Suddenly everyone heard the voice; indeed none could avoid it. It was loud, staccato and aggressive, this public rendition on the mobile phone. With only one half of the conversation audible, much imagination was called into play as I tried, like many, to interpret the other. Totally oblivious to the forest of eyes that were fixed upon him, he pursued with vigorous intent the one who clearly had affronted him.

"Abdullah, is that Abdullah? Well, never mind, just get me the driver of carriage 263. What do you mean, you can't find him? He must be there, he told me to ring at this time. You sure your name's not Abdullah? I should think so, you ought to know your own name. Friday, what about Friday? I never said Friday, its Tuesday. Well, will he or won't he? Well, 9090 you should know, I can't help that. It's nothing to do with me!"

Looking towards those of us who were clearly engrossed with what was going on and expressing some degree of impatience, he summed it all up with that institutional arrogance of the typical Englishman abroad, "How can you do business with these people? They don't even speak English!" The trouble was he was German.

Did we really order all that?

Everything about them told you that they had just arrived and it had been a rush to get to the pool. Clearly that is where they wanted to be. A relaxed attitude overtook them as they settled down on the loungers. Quickly it dawned on them that almost all the other occupied loungers had hotel towels on them, so she sent him off to find out what system was in place. Returning, he was followed by the pool attendant carrying rolled up towels. Quickly their loungers were covered. "Will that be four Sir, one for lounger and one to use to dry yourself?" Sir, found his wallet, but only after a few moments because it was in the poolside bag and otherwise he was pocketless. By the size of the tip it would be four and the exchange was greeted with many smiles, clearly anticipating more days of the same to come.

Organising themselves now engaged them and because it was their first time to be there, it took some time. Not everything that was needed was present and not everything present was needed. Each had a book but as yet the pages would not stay turned indicating that neither had yet been started. Each thought the other had brought a small personal towel but in the event there was only one. "Darling I'm sure I've left my make-up in the room. It's not in my bag or yours." So the confusion of the first visit to the pool began to be exposed. "I really must take more care tomorrow. These colours are all wrong together and I'm sure people will notice."

Now, as they relaxed they began to realise that the last meal they had enjoyed had been on the aeroplane and though it had not been totally unpalatable, it did have a long way to go to be classed as satisfying. "Do they serve food at the poolside dear?" she questioned him. Almost before the question had passed her lips he was on his feet. Heading for the Poolside Bar he waved without turning his head, the implication being that he had understood and did not need more eye contact at this stage. Finalising the arrangement of all the belongings they had carried to the pool, for the umpteenth time, she lay down supinely to await his return. In his hand he carried a menu which he gave her with a satisfied air of something really accomplished. They were going to be able to eat at the poolside and on the loungers.

She perused it, he perused it, and together they began to say what each felt they would like. Silently and unannounced, from behind the loungers, a waiter appeared with towel hanging limply over his arm. Eager to take their order he made his presence known as he bowed towards them. "She would like this and I would like that, and can we have extra here and some water with ice?" How could the poor man carry all that in his head? Yet that was his skill for, as he made his way back, he took another order from another couple, though I surmised it was for a drink only.

Now, relaxed with everything sorted, they could begin to talk. Indeed there was a great deal to talk about too. Surprised, I overheard her ask what his wife would think if she could see them now. So much more began to fall into place. The hinted embarrassment and uncertainty was now explained. However, my musings were interrupted by the approach of not one, but three waiters. The first two bore the food whilst the third was in charge of the ice bucket and the water.

"Darling! We didn't order all that did we?"

Still much left to learn I fear.

The Tattooist's Trade

Near to where we live a Tattooist plies his trade. Am I the only one that thinks this strange primeval art is seeing something of a renaissance? Was not the Ice Man, deep frozen on his walk across the Alps so many centuries ago, adorned with skin punctures filled with pigment? Was not the serious suggestion made that the pattern of his tattoos marked out some placement points for the acupuncturist to exploit his art?

Sometimes the activities of antiquity do enjoy successful revival. Maybe the most famous and written about tattooed mummy of Ancient Egypt is that of Amunet, a priestess of Hathor, who displays with blue-black dots and dashes several lines and patterns about her person.

It is both the canvas and the pattern that command attention. Hence my reference to our neighbour, who for canvas, uses the East facing wall of his end-terrace house. There is no square inch of it that has not been given over to a display of his art and I guess, it is part of his portfolio from which you might care to choose a scaled-down version of his combatant dragons. When, however, the canvas becomes the human skin, how do you choose what should be seen and what hidden? Fully clad there is no clue what lies beneath the clothing but as layer by layer, each garment is divested, more and more is exposed to see the light of day.

So it was that afternoon. Enjoying the heat of the sun at the poolside and allowing the soporific effects of lunch to take its course, I slid in and out of that enjoyable state between wakefulness and sleep where dreams so often intervene as well. Not many loungers away, newcomers arrived and began to settle themselves. As custom demands, the first activity is to undress. By years, I would have put them in their seventies, but such are the addendum's applied to the human body by science that looks can be deceptive in establishing accurate age. With the initial activity now over it was time for the anointing to begin. With some relish he began the process which clearly would take some time for he had much ground to cover. Lapsing into shallow sleep, I was left with the image of the circular motion of his hands, but on awaking he was still busy and I wondered for how long I had dozed when suddenly I noticed that she had turned over. I looked again and saw that he was giving very close attention to one particular spot. I say spot but I should really have said area. It was her thigh and it was vast. At first I thought he was trying to clean something off but here there was no thick beach oil to attach itself to the skin. Looking again, through my half closed eyelids, I saw that there was pattern to this abstraction. It was a pristine tattoo. My eyes did not allow me to focus sufficient for an accurate identification, however it appeared to involve some ankhs (an Egyptian cross with loop at top) and an eye of Horus (Symbol of protection). Drifting in and out of sleep again I got to wondering for whose benefit this decoration might have been applied, for it was so positioned that, save when the swimming costume was worn, the only other spectator would be the one who seemed to be giving it such attention now.

The Waiter's Hair

When there is not a great deal of hair remaining, you have to do your best with what you have left or as some would say, make the most of a bad job or again, make a little bit go a long way. There is of course, the totally shaved head, which goes against all that. To disguise the fact that the genes have given you a bad deal as far as adornment of the head is concerned, the head is completely shaved to give the impression of complete baldness. Is there more sympathy for a head totally devoid of hair than for those that sport sparse growth? Various ways have been devised to address the problem and a rich variety of styles are discernible if you cast your eyes about. Some grow what is left on the left and sweep it right and some grow what is left on the right and sweep it left, whilst yet others grow the back very long and sweep it forward. I have yet to see the reverse of this where the front is grown long and swept back. That could well be a genetic impossibility for the follicles.

I have however to admit that it was in Egypt that I saw the epitome of tonsorial sculpture, the very opposite of those creations worn by the Sumo wrestlers whose hair thickness seems to be exaggerated with false pieces and built to withstand much pounding. This gentleman, well groomed in his perfectly fitting uniform, moved with grace and charm, tray aloft, full or empty, like some choreographed exponent of the balletic art, among chairs and tables, scattered in nonchalant style around the vast reception area. It was as he bent low to move the contents of tray to table or visa versa that it first struck. It needed close observation of several encounters to determine of what this particular coiffure comprised. Single or double crowns are by nature left or right, off-centre but always towards the back. This fine example however, sported a crown in the very centre, right on the highest pinnacle of the crown of his head. Equal lengths of fine jet black hair, almost appearing to have been waxed, radiated from this fulcrum and dispersed in symbiotic precision, uniformly spreading around that magnificent tonsure, exposing the lace-like pattern of white flesh beneath.

Temptation was immense, just to grasp that tiny gathered bun of black. All the precision would be lost and hours of labour all to no avail, would have been forfeited. I did not succumb, for it was fear that gripped me. What if the whole arrangement was, with some superglue, attached to skin and scalp, that might not be released should my grip be of such strength.

Fit Forever

With the grace of gazelle, whose images are etched 'in perpetuity' upon so many of the rocks of the Eastern Desert, she moved from height to height with sure-footed bearing. Age was never an issue, whether it was on the tennis court or on steep desert inclines. As one was sure, taking the ball on true trajectory, so the other was accomplished with rough, ragged rocks of indescribable sharpness. Yet both had to submit to steady tread and sure-footed stability and this of an octogenarian!

Guileless of character and such a fun companion with which to travel, she had one other secret hidden talent which all fellow desert lovers envied. From whatever height, from whatever distance, whatever the obstacles and whatever the time, though you may be standing next to the selected lunch site, as soon as the call, 'Lunch is ready,' echoed around the wadi cliffs, she would be first to the tables, ready with paper plate poised to receive from the said tables of the desert's delights.

How we loved the banter, loved the fun and how to a man and a woman, we envied the agility.

Kharga Water Snake

Kharga Oasis is Egypt's centuries-old place of banishment, once for dissenting Christians at Bagawat and now for dissenting politicians and other activists that are housed in the maximum-security prison that has acquired the nickname 'Scorpion'. For those of us not banished but who come willingly, there is a hotel going by the name of The Pioneers and it too has earned a nickname. We call it the 'Pink Palace,' which has solely to do with its colour! Who it is pioneering, what and why, is something of a mystery.

Not long after it had opened, it was our delight to sample its services. We were only a small party and thought we were the only guests, that was until dinner was served, when we discovered we definitely were! With more than a hundred rooms, it is an imposing structure for its location and once inside you almost find yourself asking for a room upgrade with a Nile View. Palatial, is the word that comes to mind for both bar and rest rooms, though the limited stock of one was equalled by the limited stock of the other. Situated next to each other there was ease of access down a darkened passageway that separated the two. Changed from desert clothes for dinner and eager for the one, yet knowing I needed to avail myself of the other first I headed towards it.

Each marble adorned cubicle was inviting and I selected one, though not aware of any outstanding, particular criteria. The hotel restrooms usually have a little man, often dressed in that ubiquitous coverall, the faded blue galabeya, who in exchange for a grubby one Egyptian Pound offers a sheet of pristine paper. However, he was not to be seen on this occasion. I quickly closed the door, which to my surprise could be securely fastened from the inside, and thereupon relaxed. Some moments later I cast my eye around searching for the white roll, only to be disappointed. It was at that moment I realised in my hurry to change for dinner, I had forgotten the Egyptian traveller's golden rule, 'never leave your room without a pack of paper hankies'. Yes, it was too late!

All however, was not lost, for there beside me was the flexible hose. Upon examination its operation looked simple enough, just squeeze a small lever and all would be well. On reflection I should have done an operational check first but, eager to be in the bar, I took strategic aim and activated the device. Now, to say that it had a mind of its own would be an understatement, for as though without warning, and I certainly was not prepared, a powerful jet of freezing water hit a tender spot! I stood upright at remarkable speed and of course let the offending apparatus go. For a moment my mind thought that, if I let the lever go the water's flow would automatically stop. How wrong I was. Pressure was abundant and the hose thrashed about uncontrollably, sending a stream of water forth which flew in every direction. In vain I tried to grab the offending device behind the head, as one was taught to handle snakes but all to no avail. Uppermost in my mind now was exit strategy. First I had to understand the scene. I had yet had no time to raise my trousers even to half mast. With the writhing snake now firmly under one foot, water continued its vigorous flow across the floor. To my great relief no one else had entered yet so I was still alone and so a plan emerged.

Spying a pipe-joint near the ground I managed to wedge the hose under it in such a way that the force of the flow held it in place. Next I raised my trousers. To say they were wet would be an understatement and they were also cold. I did up the top button to hold everything in place and pulled down shirt and jacket to create as normal look as possible and retraced my steps along the aforementioned corridor. Entering the bar, which thankfully had very concealed lighting, I noticed a line of eight very softly upholstered chairs. I swear the barman saw me sit down upon the first, for he only had one other customer with which to contend. Pressing myself down on the chair as hard as I could to squeeze out as much water as possible, I began to repeat the process moving from chair to chair. Next time the barman looked I had got to number five. By number eight the wetness behind had diminished to a tolerable dampness and I hoped the dinner table chairs would be upholstered too as I was not yet ready for a plastic topped one. Looking around as casually as I could I noticed a man emerge from the corridor wielding a squeegee, maybe believing, that with this broom, whose bristles had been replaced with a stiff rubber scraper he could stem the flow. If it was Arabic he was shouting, I could do an immediate translation. 'For someone's sake, get another squeegee and help me stem this tide'.

Bahariya Massage

It was at Bahariya Oasis that we met the Doyen of the Desert, Cassandra Vivienne, who had lost the title, 'Queen of the Desert' in this very place, but that is a story for another time. Her book, in its several revised editions, 'Islands of the Blessed', is an inspiration to all who think that Egypt is just the Nile and its adjunct, the Red Sea. Her knowledge of the Oases is encyclopaedic and should you happen to meet her and there is time, encourage her to tell family stories. She is just full of them. Her delightful wit shines through her eyes and can captivate the unwary. Enough though, of that, I must get to the story of the massage.

Sometimes out of wine and sometimes out of masseurs, the 'Hotel', clustered around a hot spring, full of rusty minerals, is a very pleasant place. You are sure of the warmest of welcomes but that could depend upon your gender. However, on this occasion the services of a masseur were available, yet, far more importantly, or so he said, was the new consignment of Siwa olive oil that had just arrived. In his opinion there was none finer and as it had a scarcity value, we should all avail ourselves by signing up on the waiting list at once. So it was that I came to be persuaded.

Never had I previously contemplated such an experience. I felt I was far enough from home to take the risk. No, I would not go for the first slot but rather second or third but in the event I was the first. "What should I wear?" was a question I asked myself and decided on my swimming trunks and a loose T-shirt. Very tentatively I knocked on the door which was a fraction open and which gave way, even to my gentle touch. There I saw him.

He was huge, towering above me with biceps bigger than my thighs. How puny I felt as with one motion he had divested me of my shirt and fearful for my trunks, I found myself lifted high in the air and placed upon the table. This being my first and only experience of this sort, I was full of apprehension.

Beginning at the back of my neck, as I lay on my stomach, the warm Siwa oil flowed and he began to work his fingers and thumbs deep into my flesh. Little was overlooked as once more, with a flourish, he turned me quickly over and gave attention to what he could not reach from the other side. In a little under ten minutes it was all over. As I emerged and cautiously walked back to the hot pool for a medicinal dip, I felt all eyes were focused on me as though all were expecting that something strange and terrible had happened to me. I nodded to the next in line and she made her way towards the penitential room. As we passed, to give her confidence, I said that it was great. The look in her eyes seemed to be expressing some doubt. After ten minutes had elapsed, the third in order on the list began to make preparations.

After another ten minutes some apprehension became apparent. What were they doing in there? When a further ten minutes had elapsed and the door had not opened the third in line took the decision that it was not for her. It was a further fifteen minutes before my successor emerged, and avoiding eye contact, looked for number three on the list only to find that with four and five, all had escaped.

Mersa Matruh

If travelling to Siwa, perhaps the most famous of all Egyptian Oases, from Cairo, you have to pass through the famous battlefields of El Alamein. Respect means that you pause and view what has been prepared for you to see. As one who was a child when all this was happening, I was eager to see what was there. It was the cemeteries that had the most profound effect. Multitudes, standing row upon row, of graves marked out with stark white crosses, came as a shock. Is this what it was all about? So long ago and now the foes are friends and at least here, war has ceased. But why did all die so young? Through reluctant tears that I don't want anyone to see, I read names and ages and call to mind that far away my grandfather was cut down by a sniper's bullet, depriving me of meeting him whose name I was chosen to perpetuate. What of these and their children's children? Are they remembered as others bear their names?

On from there, for mile after mile, the road takes you past hundreds of hotels and holiday villages and you are left wondering whence all the people could possibly come, to fill these acres of development, month after month. It takes a while before the environs of Mersa Matruh are sighted, all of 300 km from where that decisive battle of World War II raged. By now it is toilets that are the most urgent need and the drivers of our small convoy of 4x4s are made aware with rapidly growing urgency.

We sweep through the town not knowing where we might come to rest. There are many anxious faces. With great relief for all we eventually stop, only to discover we are at the local police station and not at the public toilets. Negotiations are entered into and we are invited to climb out, courtesy of the local constabulary, who have kindly offered us free use of their facilities. Chivalry dictates that the ladies are given priority and we watch them disappear into a maze of buildings. Minding our own business and awaiting our turn, the peace is shattered by cries of distress.

"That was terrible, I'll never do that again!"

"When I came out of the cubicle all I could see was a row of men's backs and as I screamed they all turned and looked at me. I just ran for my life!"

"How on earth do they expect you to sit up on those silly little things anyway, they were far too high!"

The kindness of the police was more appreciated by the men than the ladies. That force had no provision for equality of women members as none as yet had been recruited.

SHUT UP!

The arguments began and the Kalesh drivers were taking sides. One had overtaken another, stolen his fare, gone to Karnak Temple and now come back to base. Gesticulations gave way to verbal assault that the untrained ear did not understand and that is probably just as well. It sounded as though it was getting very nasty. The volume rose another few decibels. More Kaleshes stopped, attracted by the noise. Again the volume rose.

The rear of the hotel overlooked the street corner and the scene was highly visible from my third floor balcony. All labelled Nile View balconies in the brochure, they began to be peopled by the tourists drawn by all the 'fun' below. It seemed as if the hapless driver was heading for a lynching.

Then suddenly, from about the fifth floor came the most almighty roar you could ever have heard. "SHUU-------UT UP!" rang round and round echoing off the high hotel walls. Quickly it reverberated down to street level.

Instantly there was silence everywhere. All looked around to see from whence that fearsome noise erupted. The drivers looked at each other then at the horses. The tourists looked down and the drivers looked up and silence reigned. All began quietly to disperse.

I had no idea that I could shout that loud.

Could it be a Film?

She sits on a chair in the full glare of the sun, loosely wrapped for protection against its burning rays. Only a small waistline is exposed as well as a face half hidden by the darkest pair of shades. Slim would be one description, skinny would be another. The poolside attendants fawn. She rises gracefully and moves with catwalk elegance to a place of complete shade where she hides under a thick blue towel. Only a film star seeking to draw attention to herself could behave like that.

Precocious children appear. Numerous young ladies in jumble sale dresses move to and fro. Loud voices are heard over two-way radio systems, and then: "Quiet on the set!"

Something is really going down here. Clearly they can only be actors. (Is it the most self-indulgent occupation upon earth?) Some are dressed in an Egyptian style with hair and heavy jewellery to match. A Howard Carter figure with full head of hair stands to one side as though waiting for an appointment. Slowly it dawns. The BBC has arrived. Directors, set designers, actors, actresses, costume co-coordinators and a host of hangers-on all seem to be doing something but I don't quite know what.

"What's going on?" I ask?

"A film about Carter and Tut for the Beeb."

But is the lithe, dark-skinned beauty involved? I continue to muse. The Carteresque figure returns with hair and side burns trimmed, looking far more at ease with himself. The lady behind the shades still remains a mystery.

It is March and Luxor is warm. The breakfast touched a

spot and now it is time to perform the ritual anointing at the poolside. Lying back on the lounger, even at that early hour in the morning, drowsiness descends and slowly the eyes close.

What the dream was about I cannot recall clearly, but as my eyes begin to focus, there is Lord Carnarvon, Howard Carter, and Theodore Davies. In close conversation they are gently strolling, not up the incline of the Valley of the Kings, but past the foot of my lounger.

Have I been transported back in time? I rub my eyes. I am still at the poolside of the Egotel Hotel. So what in the world is going on?

Before long all becomes clear. The BBC is making a new series of films for transmission in the autumn. The discovery of Tut's Tomb, the exploits of Belzoni and Champollion's work of deciphering Hieroglyphs, is to be the subject matter for a series of six programmes.

"Would you like to be an extra?" is the next question.

"Yes, if that's possible," I reply, having visions of at last being discovered.

"The beard is fine, Sir, its just the age that's a problem."

"Ah, too old," I sigh.

No one even stops me in the street now to seek my views for the Opinion Polls. All I could do was to watch the characters move from the wardrobe to the dressing room, then on to the decrepit hotel next door, in whose bowls Tut's Tomb had been recreated. Now it was possible to move behind the buildings parallel to the Corniche without ever venturing on to it, thanks to a series of footbridges over the back walls. This meant those who were about to be filmed were spared the usual banter of 'Excuse me,' 'Where you from?' 'Where you going?' 'Felucca?' 'Kalesh?' 'Good price,' and 'Market today.'

Les Misérables

Uncertain as to which oriental country they hailed from, I made some enquiries. It turned out to be South Korea. There were nearly eighty in this party and it was by all accounts the first visit to Egypt for them all. Arriving late at night they had been processed by reception and ushered to their rooms. Breakfast was an experience they seemed to enjoy but it was the hour that haunted them. Along the Corniche the coaches stood in serried ranks, engines running. Apparently it is impossible to turn them off. At 6 a.m. the hotels disgorged their overnight occupants, who spilling onto the road, begin to fill the coaches. Then comes the drive to the bridge for those heading to the Valley of the Kings or along the Corniche for those going to sample the delights of Karnak Temple. At each destination our coach-load would join the other fifty or more coach-loads and the scrum and mayhem of the day began.

To hear your guide, to see the site, to locate a point of interest, was not so much an effort as an exploit, that then turned into an adventure. On the return leg, the assault course of the vendors was faced. They, who force their wares upon the unprepared, began to rub their hands with glee upon seeing such a multitude. Then there was the heat. It went unnoticed to begin with, but as the day unfolded and the legs began to take the strain, as the water bottles emptied, not always down the throat, the pleasant warmth began to assume greater proportions and the sweat became a nuisance. The will to stand alone and unaided gave way but hieroglyphs on no account could be leaned upon.

Relief came as the air-conditioned coach began its journey to the next itinerated scene. So it was repeated as the day wore on. Again the welcome hotel beckoned and a bed to lie upon was a vision of nirvana. At the appointed time, dinner was ready to be consumed. And in they came, ushered by a guide, assuming they were all hard of hearing, shouting directions in a language only they could comprehend. This could have been a cast from a colourful production of Les Miserable as their faces told the story of the day.

Taking up Arms

'A pacifist by nature and conviction.' Do not let these words deceive you. Security and safety can cover a multitude of sins. When travelling on the Nile cruisers, discretion is a watchword and the guns along with those who wield them, are not so noticeable. The unwary passenger may run into a uniformed and armed man from time to time but for Egypt that is all part of the scene. It is when it comes to the smaller cruisers that security gets interesting.

At 07.00hrs prompt the 'Lotus' slips its mooring alongside the Iberotel and reverses out into midstream. Steadying course the captain applies the power and the little boat gathers speed. Heading north with the current, rank upon rank of moored cousin cruisers are past, as is the Luxor Hilton and soon the moored Seaplane is approached. Without any warning our vessel slows but no one seems disturbed. Do we have a malfunction, have we left something or someone behind or is there something about to happen? I fear the latter.

Commotion on the right hand bank signalled by the siren of a police launch seems to say that something is amiss. At a leisurely pace we are approached and it becomes clear that the launch is equipped with a boarding party. Drawing up to our stern port-side, both vessels adjust speed and move forward in tandem. On the given signal we are boarded, first by two uniformed Nile Navy Marines, if that is the name by which they go. When they are settled a process of transference begins. Hand over hand, first a pair of wheels, about half a metre in diameter. These are followed by some heavy boxes and then comes the 'pièce de résistance' as I heard it described, a heavy machine gun.

The full boarding party climbs aboard our cruiser, some six more sailors in all. Without any fuss and much quicker than it came, the launch moves off, we gain speed and the episode is almost over. Leaning over the upper deck, the scene below could grace the finest of Ealing comedies. The gun is mounted on the wheels, the boxes that contain the ammunition are set to one side and then the wheels are lashed to our boat with some slender rope or heavy string. I am left to wonder if this system has ever been tested. What would be the effect of the recoil? My mind goes back to basic training, albeit in the Royal Air Force, of lying in the prone position on the range with a Bren gun in my hand. 'Single Shot' the sergeant said, 'Fire!' But alas, I pulled the trigger, only to realise that I had not set my gun to 'single shot' and before I knew it my magazine was empty.

Group Travel

They come from a variety of nations; they vary considerably in numbers, and they arrive at a variety of times. They are the 'bread and butter' of the hotels, guaranteeing room occupation and giving a good guide to the number of those attending dinner. Making your way through them at reception when you are valiantly trying to get attention can be frustrating. After dispersal all returns to its sedate normality but you really have no idea who is enjoying the delights of the establishment.

Come dinnertime and that is another matter. Most groups come down reasonably early and on this particular occasion there were only half a dozen other guests enjoying the 'Italian Evening'. Previous conversation with the waiters had alerted me to the fact that the long row of central tables was for a party and we were wondering from whence they might come. Soon they began to pour in and it was clearly apparent that the Orient was the place of origin, with the likelihood of Japan being the country. Greeted by the head waiter, they were asked if they were part of a group and subsequently directed to the aforementioned tables. Whether they all understood or not didn't seem to matter for all followed the general direction.

The exception to this was when a large elderly Caucasian gentleman, accompanied by a rather demure smaller lady, whom I took to be his wife, entered the dining hall mingled in with the other guests. "Group Sir?" was the greeting. "No, young man," was the reply as both continued on their way. Only a matter of yards away they were again greeted.

"Group Sir?" "No young man," was again the response but this time the decibels increased a tad. Now a third waiter approached from an adjacent table and yet again put the same question. Patience was scarce now. "No, I am not a group. I thought you could see that," was the reply issued in even louder tones. Alas there was more to come. Yet one more waiter was unfortunate enough to ask the same question for the fourth time. "No, I am not a Group. Isn't it obvious that I am not a Group? Do I look like a Group? Do I look as though I have anything in common with your Group? The questions were thrown with ever increasing speed, volume and a liberal helping of expletives.

By now his poor wife was looking very embarrassed and sought refuge at a corner table just for two. As he sat down I was reminded, by his features that I may have seen him somewhere before. From time to time these thoughts invade the mind and it is almost impossible to shake them off until the nagging query is resolved. It was not until later, when I was back in my room that I was moved to research the resemblance. Reaching for my Guide Book of African Birds I turned the pages to find the beautiful depictions of the Eagles. There he was, a Martial Eagle in his entire splendour and certainly not in a group.

The Boy and the Buoy

The boy was waiting at the buoy and the fact that it was not in the water but on dry land did not seem to bother him one little bit. There was some water fairly close, indeed a lot of water, if truth be told. The Nile is in full spate, disgorging, so the locals say, more water than for fifty years. But what, I wondered was attracting him? Looking this way and that, the impression he gave was confusing. He could be waiting for someone to come but on the other hand he could be waiting until he was absolutely certain no one else was about.

The Mosque Call to Prayer had come and gone. It was Friday, also it was the season of the fast of Ramadan and the location was Dendera. The loud speakers on the Mosque were still quivering. Ours was the only boat tied up at the makeshift dock and the passengers had all disembarked for a visit to the magnificent Temple dedicated to the goddess Hathor. It would be a two-hour wait and rest would be denied as the minaret was but a hundred metres away.

Sitting watching the birds come down to drink and bathe at the river-edge from the upper deck of the boat, I saw the boy again. This time he was beginning to undress. The galabeya was discarded, the sandals put to one side and the football shorts, appearing to support Arsenal, were readjusted. It was then I realised he, like the birds, had come down to the river to bathe. Either he was waiting for companions or he wanted to be alone. Exposure to the sun at noon did not seem to bother him, yet still he waited.

Some perorations from the preacher's voice echoing forth from the mosque minaret found a resonance with me. I closed my eyes and was transported to a different place. The little Welsh Chapel was full to overflowing and the preacher had reached 'Joel,' where a poetic flow of words controlled the preacher rather than he control them. Strange, I thought, the Imam and the Revivalist, both preaching their hearts out and both in a language I could not understand and neither would they have been able to understand each other, yet sounding remarkably alike in extolling the merits of a virtuous life.

Back to the boy by the buoy. Just in time too. Having removed himself about ten yards from the raised docking point on which the buoy rested, he turned about and ran, as though his life depended on it, towards the water, launching himself, as with grace and poise he descended with a dive worthy of a competition, hardly disturbing the surface of the Nile as he entered its cooling waters. Rising, he swam towards some rocks, hoisted himself onto them and began to allow the sun its drying task.

Now his wait is over. The mosque disgorges its youth. Running, they too reach the waters' edge and wave and greet their friend. He swims over to join them. One or two are carrying boxes that look remarkably like those given to us in lieu of breakfast when we left the hotel to start our trip. Indeed they are. Some of the Temple party gave them to the boys as they were entering the mosque and now they are free to explore the contents and enjoy the feast. However, they have reckoned without their friend who skipped the prayers to take a swim. Cuffing them about the ears, he points out to them that this is the season of the Fast, for with scowls and cries, they repack the boxes and setting them aside for after sunset, undress ready to throw themselves into the deep waters of high Nile and enjoy a swim.

Is there a moral here that he who skips prayers holds, with greater tenacity to the tenants of the faith, than they who religiously observe the rites?

The Hat

Period dramas have a fascination all their own, not least in giving insight into the lives of the long dead. What they wore, particularly on their heads can often be intriguing.

They only thing that was missing as she approached the pool was a parasol, held at the appropriate angle to balance the dainty steps. Never again would she see her seventieth year however much she hotly disputed it. For a moment I thought the lounger would be too low but with sheer elegance she lowered herself to a sitting position and then to a reclining one, as she tested the angle of adjustment already chosen for her by the poolside attendant. He was still hovering, no doubt expecting an enhanced tip, as she invited him to allow her another towel. Upon her head she wore a black hat with a broad brim, which she did not remove even when she was ensconced in shade. Why it was that I took notice of the hat didn't at first register with me. When it did, I realised that it was the fact that her whole demeanour and movement was governed by the hat. Where was it that I had seen this before? I began to think. Yes, the memories began to return and I could see them.

It was that first trip to 'The Warm Heart of Africa', as she styles herself, or to others simply Malawi. There it was that I first encountered women whose role it is to labour in the fields, in the homes and with the children wrapped upon their backs, then to wait upon the men. If ought is to be carried, it has to be upon the head and what I have not seen upon the head? She put down the wood that had taken her all day to find and walking over I tried to lift it. I could not, whereupon she called a friend and together they raised the branches. Working her way along underneath them, she adjusted her head position and soon was off on her own, perfectly balancing something too heavy for me to even lift. Food, cooking pots, tools, washing bundles, water, vegetables and fire, I have seen all carried on the head, and more often a child has been secured in a shawl on the back as well. With a burden on her head, her whole deportment is controlled by that fact, and her posture is perfected.

This is what I was seeing again at the poolside. The whole body posture determined by what was balanced on the head. In this case a black hat. This fashion accessory was doing for her bearing what the burdens of necessity did for the women in Malawi. Distracted for some moments, I turned again in her direction and she had gone. Looking around I failed to see her until, that is, I looked across the pool. There she was, as far as I could tell, for all I could see was a black hat moving over the surface of the water. What sort of glue had been used as a fixative and would she ever be able to get it off crossed my mind?

Videos, Visas, and a Pen

Airports are places of perplexity. I am thinking of those less familiar ones and those where the procedures vary from officer to officer. Some will remember Luxor when it was almost more military than civil, at least you would think so with such vagaries of security. All the uncertainty of what was expected from standing orders had not really percolated down from the confusion that was Cairo.

It was the visa that came first. He couldn't find it in my passport and told me, by gesture, to wait at one side, at least that is how I interpreted it. After a while, he arrived with another, whom I assumed to be his superior. He went through my documents and was as perplexed as his junior. This meant that the superior of the superior of the junior would be needed.

I have found that it always pays to be polite and submissive at border entry and exit points. My worst experience was at the border between Malawi and Mozambique, which was a simple pole straddling a track. We snuck in along this ill-defined forest track where at the border, a civilian policeman wrote our nine names, spelt phonetically, on a piece of scrap paper, which he proceeded to give us and explained to our Chechewa speaker that we should surrender it on our return.

All was fine until we came to a forest bridge spanning a narrow gorge at least ten metres deep. This comprised some sturdy branches placed lengthwise across this small but steep-sided stream. We decided to risk driving the vehicle over and got three parts of the way when one of the branches moved. Having all got out and 'walked' across the remaining branches, that is except for the driver, we began to ponder our fate. About five minutes passed before there were at least ten strapping men emerging from the bush who lifted the vehicle on to another of the wooden supports and we were once again on our way. The dilemma we faced was not how to get to where we were going but rather how to get back from whence we had come. The bridge was now impassable from the other direction.

Another forest track, another pole bridge to cross and alas another border policeman too. Yes, and he was not a kindly Malawian but an aggressive Mozambican. For not having crossed at his point and because neither we, nor he could understand the paper we produced, a summary fine of $100 per person was issued. There was no way that we had $900 so the long wait began, punctuated by negotiations from time to time. Three hours later the deal was struck. At $10 a head we thought we had a good one and how glad we were to see that pole straddle the track behind us.

So finally, the superior of the superior of the junior did allow me to point out that my visa was in my passport. The problem was that the style was new and issued in London. No one at Luxor had yet seen one like it. All the booths, two in those days, ceased to function as my passport was passed around for close inspection.

Before the rules were changed, you had to register your video camera on entering Egypt and each new design format was a cause of special interest to the customs officials. The call went up and as my new video camera was held aloft the custom officers gathered around. I had to show them how it worked but was not allowed to take a picture of them because of 'security'. Woe betide if you left your video camera in the cubicle provided for it at The Valley of the Kings and then forgot to collect it. Your arrest at the airport would be watched by all your friends.

Departing was almost complete. An official, of what or doing what I do not know, approached me. He ominously reached out his hand towards my chest. I wondered for a moment what he was going to do to me. Then I remembered. As I had completed the entry form and secured it in my passport, I returned the pen to the top pocket of my jacket. Gleefully he retrieved it from my pocket and smiling, he said, 'My Pen.'

Changing Rooms

With the temperature, day after day, hovering around a hundred on the old Fahrenheit scale, the pool is the most welcome place, if you are prepared to run the gauntlet from the air-conditioned room and make a dash for it. The fact that everyone else tries to escape there makes for quite a crowd, not only in the pool but occupying the loungers. Groups of friends gather here and there and the world is put to right repeatedly.

The same group of four is there every day and never seem to run out of topics of conversation. It usually focuses on news from home, in this case the UK. However, on this day a fifth member, who clearly seemed to be updating them with news of one sort or another, joined them. You cannot fail to hear what she is saying and the longer she goes on the more interested I became. "It's like this', she tells them. 'We arrived at the hotel and were shown our room only to find that when we got there the air-conditioning was not working. We asked if we could be given another room and they agreed saying they had several not in use. When we got to the fresh room, I did the first thing that I always do and rolled back the sheets to see if they were clean, well you would, wouldn't you? They were not at all clean."

She went on to say that there were three things that made a room acceptable for her. Firstly, the air-conditioning must be working because of her chest, secondly, the sheets must be clean and thirdly, the room must be clean including the bathroom. She suggested that this was not too much to ask.

Now it was time to call the manager but he could not come.

Down to reception she said she went and demanded that the manager be in her room in five minutes or she was going to report the hotel to her travel company. The manager turned up and when she showed him the sheets he said he would have them changed. She asked about the state of the bathroom, which apparently she had explored whilst waiting for him and it was also dirty. Demanding another room she said they told her that all the rooms were fully occupied and tomorrow they would see what could be done. Clearly she was not very happy because she had already been told that the hotel was not full.

My trump card, she told them, was her husband. When I showed the manager my husband, he quickly agreed to another room change. Apparently her husband is not at all well and she said she had to tell all sorts of stories to get insurance. Under stress he looks a lot worse than he is and with me trying to sort the hotel out, she said he looked terrible. She asked for the former room, if the air-conditioning was now fixed and that seemed to be the solution agreeable to the manager.

"But that doesn't explain why we are here," she went on. In the morning I sent for the manager again. When he came I asked him what he thought of the air-conditioning and he said it seemed all right to him. "Then why," she asked again, "whenever I turn the TV on can I hardly breathe?"

Telling the manager how dissatisfied she was with the hotel she said she was going to ask the holiday company rep to place her in another. The manager suggested she borrow his phone. "That's why we are here but my husband is not well enough to come down now. But there is more. They wanted to give us a room without a Nile view! For all the trouble we've been through, that's the least that could be done."

She got what she wanted and apparently it had worked before in previous years.

The following day I needed to consult our company rep

and thankfully thought is was a different company from hers as I made my way to reception. Alas there she was, sitting in front of our rep. "There is something you ought to know "she began. "It will help you do your job better," she went on. And for the next twenty-five minutes I heard the same story from yesterday all over again as I waited my turn.

Can I Have Your Address, Please Sir?

Sometimes you wonder what qualities the selection board were looking for when they made their final choice with regard to trainee desk staff. The general feeling is that ability, willingness to learn, desire for the post and any other relatives employed, all alike take second place to looks.

The, 'Please Sir' invitation, that was so softly spoken, almost in a whisper but with the edge of breath, had my immediate and undivided attention. Not wanting to create the impression of too much interest, I rather slowly, made my way towards the desk. It was now that her looks came into play. She had them, and so discreetly wore them, it was as though she was almost reluctant to acknowledge that they had been given to her. For a moment I was completely discombobulated. "You look friendly, can you help me, please Sir?" Yet again the emphasis was on the *please* and *sir*. I could not resist. I was putty.

"It is my doctor friend. He gave me this address to write to him in England and I am sure it is wrong," she continued, offering me a piece of paper. So, I was only needed to repair a supposed rupture in a young lady's tryst. Looking at the address, she was right, it was clearly wrong. No such address as that existed. Now the dilemma had to be faced. Should I tell her of his infidelity or should I let her continue in a degree of ignorance? What had passed between them that she wanted contact and clearly he did not? Was he ending the briefest of affairs in this devious way? Had he not the courage or good grace to tell her to her

185

face, a face which to my eyes at least, could bear the epithet of beauty? What was the matter with the man? Inside the seeds of disapproval were already being sown.

"Can I have your address, please sir?" was the question that deflated every thought for this young couple that I had ever had. What on earth did she want my address for? "I'm conducting an experiment," she explained. It was her idea. Seeing so many different people from so many different parts of the world she thought to improve international relations in a very simple way. She was asking every family to send a postcard to her when they got home, saying a little bit about themselves and in return she would send one back.

"How many have you received so far?" Looking surprised she told me none, so far. "And have you sent any?" I added.

"I've been trying to send this one but I thought there was something wrong with the address", was her response.

Here was I thinking that I was going to be of service to a beautiful maiden in some distress and all she needed me for was experimental research!

Yes, I sent one. I have no idea if she received it. One however, has never arrived in return.

Blade Runner

Lying in bed, the French windows open and both sets of curtains drawn back, I looked across the Nile to the region of Meretseger, the Valley of the Kings and Hatshepsut's Temple in the far distance. Now and again, past the window, a hot air balloon would silently pursue its journey at the mercy of the gentle breeze. Now something else caught my attention that was much nearer to home. On the balcony, moving silently and secretively, were some small birds. In a few moments some larger cousins joined them and I counted seven when they were all together.

Breakfast was now necessary as the noises from the region of my stomach said that particular tank was now running on empty. Making a choice from the incredible array of bread to tempt taste buds, my eye again was drawn to something else, the crumbs. My thoughts were back with the birds and I was considering how I might get them together with these crumbs, so that I could enjoy watching them on the balcony. Collecting crumbs did not seem to be a very good idea but another thought invaded my awareness. Why not take the bread and convert it into crumbs when I got up in the morning, opening the room to the warmth of the morning and more of the magic of Egypt?

Sparrows and pigeons had a wonderful time as that holiday went by but almost as a 'thank you', the birds let me into the secret of what delighted them.

This time the venue was not the room or balcony but another favourite place of passing time. To be at the pool early is always a goal but to gain a lounger by cheating with the use of books or towels, toys or shades, is not really in my nature. Whilst many guests are up before the sun to visit the sites that abound in the neighbourhood, some seek the rest and relaxation of the pool. On this day the numbers were sparse so the choice was wide and the attendant very attentive. I settled down, opened the book, put it down, closed my eyes and soon I was lost again in that world between wakefulness and sleep. Always having difficulty in deciding which state prevails at any one time, I was aware of birds.

The bar, which guests could only access from the pool, had not yet been set out. The sunshades were not spread, the display stands were nowhere to be seen and the usual array of bottles were hidden from view. This time of day proved to be a blessing for the birds, who seeking shade, even at that early hour in the morning, flew under and upward to find a perch in the awnings covering the bars. There they could survey the scene. What they reckoned with and what I had not, was that one of the first duties of the barman in setting out his stall, was to set the air in motion by switching on the fans, set high above. Now was the opportunity for the bravest of the birds and it seemed as though they almost dared each other. Hopping onto a huge fan blade they awaited the beginning of its rotation. By centrifugal force they were flung away to begin a glide or flight as their fancy took them.

Christmas in the Red Land

An entirely new experience awaited us. For the first time ever in our married life, we were able to escape the Christmas season at home and take a holiday abroad. Leaving the cold of an English winter we set out for the warmth of Egypt which had been our destination on many previous occasions but never at this season. Living in the Inner City of Birmingham, UK, we had seen innumerable fasts of Ramadan come and go. In Egypt too we had experienced 'The Fast' many times. However, this was to be our first experience of the Christmas season in one of the homes of Islam. The first thing that struck us was the cold. Yes, December can be cold in Luxor. Just as it can be exceptionally hot with a heat wave, so also it can experience what we would describe as a cold snap. No fear of frost of course but just the thought that packing a warmer sweater would have served a very good purpose.

The journey north on the Nile towards Qena was a revelation. Dark and lurid clouds seemed to gather between the sporadic appearance of the sun, keeping the billowing black smoke issuing from the sugar refinery low to the river. Then the gentle rain, of itself a revelation was exceeded by the appearance of a rainbow. A rush to photograph the phenomenon began and conversation concerning what the Ancient Egyptians might have made of such colours in the sky, lasted some while. Those with some scant Biblical background would easily be reminded of its nature as a sign, before the much disputed flight to Egypt by the 'Asiatics.' It was as though all this had been

189

planned to make us feel at home in this distant land, at this special season of the year which, the Coptic Church of course, join in celebrating some weeks later than our Latin tradition.

Then there were the tinsel and the shining stars. How restrained it all looked when you compare it with what we have become so used to from September onwards. Here, just a hint of decoration, not the overwhelming, overdressing, of chain stores, months ahead, reminding us of the need to get rid of so much of our money and challenging us yet again, concerning our ability to repay our debt. Stars and tinsel, decorations and streamers, are not exclusive to the season here. All forms part of the colourful pageant of regular life along the banks of the Nile.

No, it was the hotel that really wrought the surprise. We, who had spent money to escape the trappings of the season were quite taken aback to find the palatial reception area given over to our decadence. There, in all its coloured tinselled and baubled glory, stood tall, a Christmas Tree. Not as large as some, but serving the same purpose, the pretence of Victorian piety, which still pervades our culture.

Sea Sick

The Red Sea had beckoned them. There was, however something about the word *sea* that caused deep seated anxiety to surface. Sea and sickness seemed synonymous. So it was that the cruise on the Red Sea was abandoned in favour of their stay in Luxor. All who have been to this remarkable city know how it can cast its spell and not only detain you but continually draw you back again, time after time.

The river not only divides the West from the East but also the North from the South. Each point of the compass holds its own fascination. East, is the place of birth and dawn, life and light, of day and activity. Here things happen and have done since the dawn of time. The Temples of Karnak and Luxor are there to bear testimony to this truth in ancient times. Try as you might you cannot exhaust the wealth of understanding that these ruins put on display. Should you want a more contemporary feel on this side of the river, you can explore the souk. Here life pulsates all around you and it seems that whatever time you may happen upon those narrow streets, there would be someone there to greet you or rather try to sell you something. All of life is for sale in this place and coupled with the pressure to buy, who has not left that maze possessing that which they did not want, having paid more than they would have liked?

On the other hand to go west across the river, is to visit the place of death and decay, night and darkness, of attempts at eternal preservation. Descend the Tombs, explore the Mortuary Temples and walk to the Worker's

Village and at every level you are confronted by the ancients' desire to live for ever. However, crossing the river is now encouraged by road rather than by ferry. Now the air-conditioned coach has replaced the open-air motor launch but I know which I prefer and it may yet return.

Going north too can be by river or road. The 'Lotus' will bear you on the river from Luxor to Qena, whilst the convoy system (though now abandoned) would take you as far as Abydos but no further. There and at Dendera you will still find the demarcation of life and death on either river bank, displayed by yet more remains of the ancients but venture south and the preferred option has to be a cruise up the Nile, save for those addicted to rail travel. Progress of the boats allows for only one description: sedate. With calm and tranquil motion you are moved placidly along the shallow channel, cut millennia before by the waters fallen as rain either around Lake Victoria or upon the Ethiopian Highlands.

She continued to explain to me why the family was in Luxor rather than on the Red Sea and I offered her suggestions for the time they would spend, saying that the hot air balloon was an experience not to be missed. Looking at her face as I mentioned, with some enthusiasm, my airborne excursion, it seemed to grow rather pale, even a 'whiter shade of pale' to borrow a title. After her next question it all began to fall into place. "Could you please recommend me a pill to prevent sea sickness when I am on the Nile?" she asked with all seriousness. "I forgot to bring any with me."

Getting the Hump!

She was somewhat short of stature, as well as having some age but as so often is the case, she was graced with great determination. If a certain tour guide was in charge of the trip, you could guarantee she would be there. If he had had a fan club, without a doubt she would have been the organising President. As it was she had to content herself with making sure that her position and status were never infringed. Whether she was a little deaf, I never did discover, but the fact was clear for all to see. She would always be found at the front of the group, standing next to the guide. Of necessity always looking up, there seemed a tenderness about her gaze, revealing perhaps more than the anticipation of the impartation of fact upon fact from the 'local expert'. If the group should pause, even for a moment, expecting a fresh view or another explanation, she would always appear at the front, yet again ahead of the game.

Speculation was rife as to just how she managed to accomplish this, time and time again. The consensus was that it would take her too long to get around the outside so she must have devised a way to go through. As her diminutive stature enabled her frequently to disappear from view, speculation was that she resorted to going on hands and knees, slipping under those who stood in her way.

The group was stationed next to a camel and all looked equally phlegmatic. Almost invisible beside the camel's hump, she had appeared and waited patiently as a number of mounting methods were demonstrated. There really was no way she was going to accomplish this feat alone so plaintively she looked around, only to despair that her favourite tour guide was nowhere to be seen. He, on the other hand was very quietly approaching her from behind. Quite suddenly, without a 'by your leave,' he hoisted her high in the air. The hump of the camel disappeared beneath her and to her amazement and that of the camel, she found herself astride the beast. There were surprised looks on both their faces and it was difficult to determine which outclassed the other in terms of self-disclosure.

Be Careful As You Sit Down

Passing the hot pool, around which the bedrooms were gathered at our lodgings in the now infamous hotel at Bahariya, the need for the services a bathroom could offer were upper-most in my mind. Vainly I tried to hurry the assistant, but as in usual Egyptian style, he had his own steady pace. At last we arrived at my room and he put the key into the lock, only to find that it would not respond to his attempts to turn it. Some very un-Arabic phrase rushed past his lips and he was gone!

I crossed my legs. On his return the door was quickly opened. A surprised look overtook his face as a tip, much larger than he anticipated was thrust into his hand, as he was hurriedly shown the door. The backpack and the holdall thudded onto the bed. By the time the bathroom was reached both arms had gained their freedom from their safari jacket and were busy loosening the belt. The lowered trousers impeded progress to the gleaming pedestal as I reversed and lowered. It was a stunning surprise, as I hit the chill seat, suddenly to be thrown sideways. Finding myself full-length upon the floor, I managed to turn over and view the wreckage I had caused. Where pipe met pan nothing was fixed, not even where pan met floor! The consequence was my rotation through ninety degrees. I was lying down and in all this excitement seemed to have totally forgotten the urgency that brought about my unexpected descent!

The Story Of My Life!

We were neither early nor late. Few had come before us judging by the number of place settings used in the dining room unless you could suggest that the staff had reset most that had been previously used. The question that would have to follow would be, 'What staff?'

The milk was missing, there were no teaspoons, side plates were scarce and what is more you only caught a glimpse of a waiter from time to time. There was no chance of getting his attention, let alone any service. The omelette station was deserted and perhaps the biggest surprise of all, there were no supervisors standing around.

By now you will have made the right assumption, I am talking about breakfast. It is nine in the morning and quite a few residents in the New Winter Palace are getting nervous. Something pretty serious must have happened to create this predicament. Maybe the ferry has broken down, capsized, or even sunk.

Fortunately none of these things are true. There must be a rational explanation for it but as yet it eludes us. The only former experience to match this was whilst attending a conference in Brighton in the UK. The hospitality at the B&B was very good and we were looking forward to another good breakfast. When we came down in the morning there was no one about and the kitchen was locked. For a while we waited in anticipation that someone had overslept and would be around very soon. Disappointed, the time for us to be on our way for the conference was fast approaching. Now some drastic measures were called for. First, we broke into the kitchen and second, because some of my culinary skill was known to one or two of the group, I was delegated to do the cooking. All this proceeded very well and everyone enjoyed what I was able to produce from what we found in the storeroom and fridge. It was not until we returned, late that same evening, that we learned what had happened. The two young men running the establishment had gone up to London for the Thursday night, as was their wont from time to time. There they had enjoyed themselves so much that they decided to stay over and travel back early the next morning but the company proved to be so entertaining that they overslept and didn't arrive back until mid-afternoon.

Alas, here, as I was approaching the omelette station with a view to getting some action going, a bleary-eyed chef approached. He had no explanation other than 'Ramadan'. Looking at each other, we began to explore this explanation but all agreed that we had heard of many things put down to 'The Fast', but surely this was stretching things a little too far. However, it turned out to be true. There was something in what the chef had said but it had more to do with the revelries of the night before, than a shadow of the season cast over another day. Once a year, in mid-Ramadan, the leading figures in the hotel chain, in this case some kind of company director, give the staff an evening of feasting and entertainment. It was a riotous and noisy affair, as we all could testify but lacking knowledge of what was going on we assumed it was a wedding party, though again the Fast should have alerted us to that one! After the food came the tombola, where each worker's entry ticket would give access to an identically numbered prize. These were of general electrical goods and later in the day we saw explanations being given about how to operate an MP3 player and various mobile phones!

All seemed very pleased with the night's work, except for the lone waiter on duty, who after I had managed to detain him for a moment, confessed that he was one of the few for whom their number in the draw had produced a blank. 'It's the story of my life!' he said in perfect English.

Invalidated Insurance

The run down from Mersa Matruh to Siwa was eagerly awaited as the 4x4s were readied. Tyre pressures were checked and rechecked, loads secured and occupants settled. The convoy of six vehicles began to move. Smooth tarmac soon gave way to sand-covered tarmac, which then gave way to sand. However, the effect of vehicles' constant use of the sand-covered tarmac was to break it up and then to corrugate it which caused considerable discomfort to drivers and passengers alike as we were bounced along.

Ever ready with solutions, the lead vehicle took to the sand alongside the fast-disintegrating surface of the highway. This made for only a slightly smoother transition but created another problem as all the vehicles followed line astern, sand being thrown up in great quantity, making visibility impossible. Now the vehicles began to move apart, spreading sideways, giving the impression of a large crab in motion. Here at least was clearer vision and therefore greater safety, one supposed.

Then murmuring was heard. Growing louder and coming from those at the back of the vehicle, the question seemed to focus on why had we left the tarmac road? A number of views were expressed but all were silenced when this retort was heard: "It's alright for you, but my insurance is invalidated if we leave the metalled road!"

This was an interesting take on insurance that was only once surpassed in my travel experience. This on a camel excursion to the ruined monastery of St Simeon next to Aswan, though on the West Bank. Arriving by motor launch at the landing stage, our small party disembarked. Looking up from the lower vantage of the river surface, little else was to be seen but the row of camels awaiting their daily excursion to the monastery, each securely held by a small boy, grasping a rope attached to the harness embellishing the animals' face. Each boy looked remarkably proud to be in charge of his family's assets.

In what seemed to be a wonderfully choreographed routine, the camels collapsed into the mounting position as we walked in single file until we arrived at our designated beast. Styles of climbing aboard varied with age and agility interspersed with fear and dread. Once all were seated, I hesitate to use the word, comfortably, the process of getting the beasts into vertical began. Encouraged by the boys using various techniques, from shouts, to sticks, to pokes, with an almost regular rhythm they all arose and began the lolloping journey.

Confidence grew, though comfort was still elusive. The boys of camel command offered the controlling rope to those perched high above, assuming they wanted to move on alone. This was the experience of the rider immediately in front of me. Innocently the boy offered up the rope to the gentleman, who had made no concession to the desert travel whatsoever. He could have stepped right into his city office, had there not been the camel between his legs, of course. Horrified, he looked down, and poured forth a diatribe of the Queen's best BBC English, of which I am positive the boy would not have understood one syllable. "Boy, don't you realise, if you let go of that rope you will invalidate my insurance!"

A big smile broke across the boy's face. Seeming to grasp the rope more firmly, the English gentlemen led his charge onward and upward across the sandy ridge. The unsteady descent to the Monastery would have made for a comical cameo, could I have but held the video still.

Two B's and a C

The two weeks sped by as they always do in Luxor. Home again and so much is forgotten. That is until the phone rang.

"Hello…. the BBC…. you're joking? You're not?"

"Could you be in London on Saturday for the 'Excess Baggage' programme? Sandi Toksvig is interviewing Joyce Tyldesley who's written the book to accompany the new BBC Egyptian series, and we'd like you to join in."

"Funny you should say that, I will be in London at the Bloomsbury Theatre for a study day about the Egyptian Delta."

"We'll send a car to pick you up."

"But wait a moment, do you know who you're talking to?"

"Well, I was given your number by someone quite reputable." (Who could that have been?)

"I have no qualifications in Egyptology. My knowledge is extremely limited. It's just that I go whenever I can."

"Just the person we're looking for, sir."

"But am I not too old?"

"Your age doesn't concern us, sir."

All these 'sirs' were getting too much.

She continued. "The car will pick you up at 9.15am at the Bloomsbury Theatre. See you at the BBC!"

The car was grand, a Mercedes. I said goodbye to my wife not knowing what might happen at the Beeb. I had heard stories! The driver did not have to know the way, all the time the car talked to him and told him when to turn and where. Oh the marvels of the great city. It seemed a long way away from the blue and white taxis of Luxor. Then again, it was!

Sandi was not at all intimidating. Tea, coffee and cookies, all from the famous kitchens I guess, were served. Joyce Tyldesley confided that she was a little nervous because the interview was going to be live. I did not tell her that my mouth was dry and I had been up all night trying to think of suitable anecdotes for the modern day traveller to the ancient land.

Ushered into the studio we were accompanied by a young man, who we discovered was the leading authority on the London Route Master Red Bus that was soon to finish its long and distinguished service in the Capital. In his hand he held his book. Just as Joyce held hers. Both my hands were full, in the left my yellow 'Post Its', covered with unreadable notes I would never need, and in the right a white plastic cup, full of water. Both were rapidly vibrating.

For fifteen minutes Joyce and I tried to look as interested as we could in the minutia of a London Bus. Then it was our turn. Joyce, fluent in all the facts and figures of those august gentlemen of a bygone era, whilst I tried to articulate why folk keep going back, and back again to Egypt.

Then it was all over. Suddenly we were on the street, going our separate ways. Joyce turned left and I climbed back into the talking Merc.

On the steps of the Bloomsbury Theatre I spotted Joyce, on her way to sign copies of her book for the study day punters. I found her again on a higher floor busy autographing. I joined the queue. Joyce looked up as she expected me to offer her a book to sign. She looked a little confused as I offered her, not a copy of her book to autograph but my pass to get into the hallowed courts of the BBC.

Later on, heading home on a red London Route Master bus, the intricacies of which I was by now very familiar with, I found myself reminiscing. When I was a boy listening to Dad's stories about Howard Carter discovering Tutankhamun's tomb in the Valley of the Kings, I told him I would go to Egypt. Now I had been many times, but never would I have imagined my adventures starting at the age of retirement!

Acknowledgements

I am grateful to my father, who really started it all. To my wife Jennifer and my son, Peter, who shared so much of the fun. To Ancient World Tours and its Director, Peter Allingham, without whom none of this would have come to pass. To David Rohl, whose continual questioning and probing of the accepted excites the mind and who, as a travelling companion, ensured order. To Dr Kent Weeks, who epitomizes generosity of both hospitality and intellect. To Janet Shepherd and the Sussex Egyptological Society for an abundance of friends. To Pan Arab Tours for all the brilliant logistical arrangements only exceeded by the amazing skills of their drivers, many of whom became loyal friends; and to my good friend and publisher Nick Corbett. Finally, any mistakes are my own, and if my memory has been faulty, I apologise. I am happy to be corrected.

Bill Dixon
Autumn 2013

Books of Interest

David Rohl
A Test of Time, London Century, 1995
Genesis of Civilization, London Century, 1998
The Lords of Avaris, London Century, 2007

Edited by David Rohl
The Followers of Horus, ISIS, 2000

Dr Kent Weeks
The Lost Tomb, Phoenix Paper Back, 1999

Dr Russell Rothe
Pharaonic Inscriptions from the Southern Eastern Desert of Egypt, Eisenbrauns, 2009

Edited by Maggie and Mike Morrow
Rock Art Topographical Survey, Bloomsbury Summer School, UCL, 2002

Dr Tony Judd
Rock Art of the Eastern Desert of Egypt, BAR, 2008

Fred Wendorf
Holocene Settlement of the Egyptian Sahara, Volume 1: The Archaeology of Nabta Playa, Springer

Cassandra Vivian
The Western Desert of Egypt, American University in Cairo

Press, Revised Edition, 2008

Daniel Jacobs and Dan Richardson
The Rough Guide to Egypt

Ahmed Fakhry
Various Oasis Guides, The American University Press, Cairo

Edited by Janet Starkey and Okasha El Daly
Desert Travellers from Herodotus to T.E. Lawrence, Astene, 2000

Wael T. Abed
The Other Egypt, Travels in No Man's Land, Egyptian Tourism Development Authority, 1998

Made in the USA
Charleston, SC
07 March 2014